Praise for Wolf's Message

"Wolf's Message is a masterpiece of intrigue. If you have ever wanted to read a book that validates immortality and communication with loved ones who have passed on, then read this book. It is an authentic portal to the other side." Caroline Myss, author of *Anatomy of the Spirit*

"To say that 'the medium is the message" may be an overly used cliché, but this medium, Suzanne Giesemann, has a message that humanity needs desperately to hear. Wolf's Message is her riveting account of how she deciphered this message from a series of clues disclosed to her by an extraordinary young man after his death – and she backs up her evidence in a way that will convince even the most hardened skeptic. This is literally a mind-blowing book. Read it and see for yourself!" Kenneth Ring, Ph.D., Professor Emeritus of Psychology, University of Connecticut, Author of *Lessons from the Light*

"For anyone interested in the afterlife, Wolf's Message is a 'must-read,' skillfully written by a very credible, enormously gifted, and highly respected medium. It is an engrossing, enthralling, engaging page-turner that will captivate most readers. This terrific book makes a powerful contribution to the growing body of compelling evidence that consciousness clearly survives bodily death and is indeed eternal. I recommend it with great enthusiasm." John R. Audette, M.S., Founder, International Association for Near-Death Studies; President, CEO & Co-Founder, Eternea & Quantrek

"Somehow, reading Wolf's Message *creates a field into which the reader is incorporated experientially. Reading, learning, and Being are rolled into a synergy that exemplifies the truths of nature and existence as they are revealed. Such authentic interactivity is rarely achieved in this context; a really good book is one in which the author draws the reader in by chronicling notions and events in such a way as to invite and affirm our ability to relate. A really great story dispenses with the dichotomy of author and reader altogether, and the precious anomaly of* Wolf's Message *is that it behaves more like an Oracle than a Book."* Barbara E. Fields, Ph.D., Executive Director, Association for Global New Thought

Wolf's Message

Wolf's Message

SUZANNE GIESEMANN

ISBN-13: 978-1-939116-99-4

A Native American grandfather is talking to his grandson about a recent tragedy in their tribe. He says, "I feel as if I have two wolves fighting in my heart. One wolf is angry and wants revenge. The other is understanding and feels compassion."

The grandson asks him, "Which wolf will win?"

The grandfather answers, "The one I feed."

~ Native American Story

Contents

Foreword

When I first learned about "Wolf," the young man celebrated in this extraordinary book, and came to understand his inspiring message "from the other side" concerning humanity's pressing need to balance mind and heart, I was reminded of Carole King's powerful song, *Change in Mind, Change of Heart*.

Released in 1991 to critical acclaim, *Change in Mind, Change of Heart* haunted my mind as it spoke to my heart, and I sang it many times. This song deeply moved me and millions of others, not only because of its beautiful melody and King's equally beautiful voice, but also because of its fundamental meaning and message about the need for us to love one another more.

Let me be blunt. The account you are about to read is one of the most beautiful, inspirational, and unbelievable yet true "stories" I have ever encountered. It has the power to change your mind as well as your heart.

To give you a sense of what you are about to read, try to imagine the following three things:

First, try to imagine that you are the parent of a young man you dearly love who is very different from most people. Your son "Wolf" (a name he adopted) believes he is living in two worlds – our conventional world of the physical, and the controversial world of Spirit. Your handsome son loves animals, poetry, and art, and he is beloved by many people. Yet he is "haunted" by mystical experiences which few of his peers share, and he has been diagnosed with schizophrenia.

Then one fateful day, out of the blue, two detectives come to your home with the tragic news that your son was struck by lightning next to a tree and killed. In an instant he is gone. Your grief is understandable and severe.

However, two days later, upon visiting your son's apartment, to your utter amazement and even greater disbelief you discover a picture drawn by your son which clearly indicates that he not only foresaw his own death, but that he specifically saw himself being killed by lightning next to a tree. [There are additional facts even more startling about his apparent death premonition which will be revealed later in the book].

How is this possible, you ask. Your world is shaken to its core.

Second, try to imagine that you are a skilled and genuine medium. You are not just any successful medium, mind you, but a medium who in your "prior life" had been a distinguished commander in the Navy. Not only were you highly educated and decorated, you were also appointed to serve as the aide to the chairman of the Joint Chiefs of Staff. In fact, along with the chairman of the Joint Chiefs of Staff, you were in the last plane to fly after the horrific terrorist attack of the World Trade Center on September 11, 2001.

Now imagine that you meet the parents of the late Wolf at a conference where you are giving a presentation on mediumship. You feel inspired to gift them a free reading, but two days before you do the reading, Wolf comes to you early in the morning, and you take reams of notes of the information he gives you. You have no idea what, if any, of this information is valid or relevant.

However, toward the end of this unanticipated "pre-reading" with Wolf, he instructs you to have the information formally "scored" by a world renowned expert in such matters. You followed his instructions, and the results turn out to be highly accurate.

How is this possible, you ask again. A deceased person was seeking you out days before the actual reading was to begin, and this was only the beginning of what would become one of the most transformative relationships in your life.

Third, try to imagine that you are a successful senior academic and scientist. You have received your Ph.D. from Harvard University; you have served as a professor at both Harvard and Yale; and you currently serve as a professor in five departments at the University of Arizona. During more than four decades of research and after more than four hundred scientific publications, your investigations have taken you from the mainstream of research to the frontiers of science, and your journey has required great perseverance, openness, and humility. You have had the privilege to test and document more than two dozen of the most gifted and famous mediums living today, one of them being Suzanne Giesemann, the author of this book.

Now imagine that one day you receive an email from this medium, claiming not only that she had experienced an unanticipated appearance of a "deceased person" named Wolf before the actual reading, but that Wolf had instructed her to have this pre-reading scored using the formal rating system you developed in your laboratory and have used successfully with this medium (and many others) on multiple previous occasions. Moreover, as you statistically analyze the careful scoring conducted by the young man's parents and validate the profound significance of this pre-reading (included as Appendix A of this book), you and your colleagues begin to have highly specific and verifiable synchronicities clearly connected to this young man during the process of Ms. Giesemann coming to know and celebrate Wolf's messages since his passing. Yes, you read this correctly.

Here is not the place to discuss these incredible synchronicities. What I can say is that they are as remarkable and revealing as the amazing synchronicities associated with Wolf as witnessed and carefully reported by the author of this book.

What you are about to read is nothing short of history in the making. The credibility of the parents, the medium, and the scientist are beyond reproach. You are not reading scientific theory or literary fiction here; the facts are genuine facts.

Professor William James, the distinguished professor of psychology at Harvard University in the early twentieth century, was quoted as saying, and I slightly paraphrase, "In order to disprove the law that all crows are black, you need only find one white crow."

James' meaning was applied specifically to mediums. He explained that all a scientist had to do was to discover and document the existence of just one genuine medium, and this disproved the "law" that all mediums are frauds. In my research reported in three books, I have had the privilege to document scientifically the existence of more than two dozen genuine "white crow" mediums.

James' same logic can be applied to "spirits." Scientific research is now beginning to document the existence of genuine "post-physical beings" who continue to care not only about their loved ones, but also their "extended family" of humanity, animals, plants, and the planet as a whole. The firm conclusion that I have drawn after carefully examining all the evidence is that Wolf is a "white crow" spirit, and that his substantial efforts and sustaining messages deserve to be honored, celebrated, and, above all, heeded.

Wolf's central message is about the essential balancing and integration of mind and heart in our evolution toward love and oneness. As you come to know Wolf and his parents, and Suzanne Giesemann and her work, and a bit about Gary Schwartz and his small contribution to this journey, I hope you will be able to experience a profound change of mind and heart.

As I complete this foreword, I find myself experiencing a beaming smile on my face and a warming love in my heart. Thank you Suzanne, and especially, Wolf.

Gary E. Schwartz, PhD

Preface

The wolf "comes when we most need guidance in our lives."

I found these words after searching for "*wolf as a sacred symbol*" on the Internet. I had recently experienced a profound close encounter with a wolf that made me want to learn more about these often misunderstood creatures. The wolf in this case was not the four-legged *Canis lupus*, however. It was a young man with a penetrating gaze who went by the nickname Wolf.

Like his namesake, Mike "Wolf" Pasakarnis was a friendly, social creature who avoided aggression. Just like his animal counterpart, the human Wolf had a strong sense of family. In fact, it was his family's desire to connect with their son after his unusual death that brought us together.

I am an evidential medium. That means that when I sit with a client to reunite him or her with a loved one who has passed, I don't share palliative messages that could apply to any grieving family member. I bring through verifiable facts that no outsider could possibly know. When such evidence comes through and is confirmed by the client, it is referred to as a "hit." Those on the other side understand that as a former no-nonsense U.S. Navy commander, I *insist* on such evidence.

Wolf surely sensed this. He didn't follow the normal rules of engagement and wait to make his presence known to me when I sat with his parents for a reading. Instead, he made an unexpected visit in the pre-dawn hours two days before the appointed session. The evidence he provided about his life was subsequently validated by his parents and rated by a noted afterlife researcher as "one of the best (visits) of its kind" he had ever seen.

Wolf came back two days later to converse with his parents through me, heaping on hit after hit that left the three of us wide-eyed at the clarity of the connection. Many of the details he provided in the two back-to-back visits were easily validated.

Because of the accuracy of the information that came through, we puzzled over a short list of words and messages which seemed to make no sense. Had his reading been a one-time glimpse across the veil, we might still be pondering the significance of those confounding clues. Instead, Wolf repeatedly made his presence known to me during the following months. Through a series of striking synchronicities which I share in this book, Wolf helped me unravel what turned out to be an intricate web that he wove during his two initial visits. The result is a profound lesson in how to find peace and balance in a world that is precariously out of alignment.

Wolf is like no other family member I have connected with on the other side. He explained in his reading that as a human he walked in two worlds at once: the physical and the non-physical. Highly connected with his spirit side in a way that others could not understand, Wolf was aware of his impending death. He not only knew how, where, and when he would die, but he predicted details of specific events that would happen in the aftermath of his transition.

Any medium who wishes to avoid the criticism of skeptics will wisely shy away from using a word such as "proof" when referring to information gained at the level of the soul. The prophetic poem that Wolf penned before he passed and the picture he drew to back up his words go beyond the mere preponderance of evidence that a good medium strives for. They constitute profound *proof* that the soul has access to information far beyond that of the human mind.

The refined vibration I felt from his spirit belied the oft-troubled young man known to his family. I have come to understand that the challenges he faced in human form were part of a greater plan. Had he lived a normal life, few would be inclined to pay attention to his message. It is the jaw-dropping circumstances surrounding his death that make Wolf's message impossible to ignore.

This remarkable story unfolded while I was on a five-month speaking tour around the United States and Canada. On that trip my husband and I visited a magical place in northern Arizona called Antelope Canyon. From the outside, one sees only a tall, narrow fissure in a facade of dull, rough rock. Stepping through the opening, the eyes blink at the abrupt shift to another world. Solid walls transform into ochre and magenta waves that flow majestically upward toward a golden light that silently beckons. In that moment when the breath stops, there is recognition that just as in life, what is on the outside often conceals the indescribable beauty within.

Wolf's Message will take you on a personal journey to the epicenter of your soul. Like stepping into Antelope Canyon, one cannot hear Wolf's story without experiencing a shift to another world. It is the world from which all of us come and to which the soul longs to return.

The wolf comes when we most need guidance in our lives. He is a teacher and a pathfinder. Wolf Pasakarnis came to bring greater awareness of our dual nature and to lead us back to the source of our own inner beauty: the heart.

He came to show us how to go home.

CHAPTER ONE

Making The Connection

Mike and Beth Pasakarnis would have preferred to remain anonymous at the *Soul Life* conference. Instead of being allowed to quietly blend in, they were singled out by medium Maureen Hancock and asked to stand.

Cameras rolled as someone thrust a microphone into Mike's hand. Maureen informed the audience that the couple had approached her at breakfast in the hotel the day before. They wanted to say hello and thank her for the reading she had given them two years earlier, shortly after the death of their son, Wolf.

"I'll never forget what you just said to me yesterday," Maureen said now in front of 250 guests. "You realized that your son is your teacher."

Mike nodded as Beth stared at the floor.

"I hope you don't mind me sharing this," Maureen said. "A lot of parents don't get to the point where you are, where you realize that your son is your guide and teacher. So could you say something about that?"

Mike shifted a bit before responding. "When Wolf passed I was completely devastated. Then we met you, and you opened up a whole new door of spiritual awareness."

Maureen zeroed in on Beth. "And Mom, I want to hear from you, too. I have given readings for so many parents with kids in Heaven, and I don't usually remember them. But I remember you, because you were scientific in your approach and you wanted facts."

Beth nodded and took the microphone from her husband. "I'm a veterinarian," she said, "so I'm a doctor and I'm science-based. I always wanted to believe in a heaven and an afterlife, but I needed proof, and you provided that proof for us."

Mike rubbed Beth's back in slow circles as she continued, "It's really turned our life around. You started the process, and Wolf has since shown us so many signs."

Beth glanced around at the sea of faces in the audience. "We would never have attended a conference like this before, I can tell you *that*," she said with conviction. The audience broke into chuckles, and then into gales of laughter when Beth muttered a sheepish, "Sorry."

Since the death of their son, Mike and Beth had been seeking answers to cosmic questions. Their search took them from their home in Mashpee, Massachusetts to Edgar Cayce's Association for Research and Enlightenment ("A.R.E.") in Virginia Beach. Until six weeks before the conference, Beth hadn't shown much interest in the books Mike had been reading about life after death. Then she had picked up a copy of *Proof of Heaven*, written by Dr. Eben Alexander, a neurosurgeon who experienced life beyond the physical world while in a coma. His words spoke to her in a unique and very personal manner. When she saw that Dr. Alexander and Maureen Hancock would both be presenting at the A.R.E., Beth suggested that she and Mike attend.

Before the conference, I was not familiar with Maureen's work, but I had read Dr. Alexander's book. When the A.R.E. staff asked me to be one of the presenters, I happily accepted. Sharing the platform with Dr. Alexander—whose credentials and demeanor define the word "credible"—would help me achieve my goal of bringing greater credibility to, and understanding of, mediumship.

My three-hour talk preceded Dr. Alexander's keynote address on Saturday afternoon. I had chosen my *"Making the Connection"* presentation, aimed at helping others to connect with Higher Consciousness. I planned to take the audience through the various levels of guidance, starting with intuition and moving on to loved ones who have passed, and from there on to spirit guides and angels.

Like Beth, who could not have imagined herself at such a conference a few years earlier, I could never have envisioned myself discussing communication with angels, let alone doing so before a large audience. Twenty years as a naval officer had left me with an over-developed "left brain." The death of my step-daughter Susan in 2006, however, caused me to ask the same kinds of questions that had brought Mike and Beth to the conference.

It was the irrefutable evidence from a medium that convinced me that Susan was still very much around. This led me to discover first-hand that consciousness operates on multiple levels beyond that which the human brain can normally perceive. When ultimately I came to realize that we all have the ability to tap into ever higher frequencies of information-carrying energy, I began a new life's work of communicating with the spiritual side of our existence. Were it not for the overwhelming quantity and quality of evidence received during those communications, I would have remained in my limited left-brain mindset. The personal experiences brought my right brain back on line, and that led me to a completely unexpected career change.

Aware that many people in the audience might be as skeptical of mediums and spirit as I had once been, I packed my presentation with evidence from the other side. To establish credibility, I began by showing a few slides from my Navy career. I flashed a picture on the screen of me with my former boss, the chairman of the Joint Chiefs of Staff. I had served a tour of duty as the aide-de-camp to the nation's top ranking officer, and I shared with the audience my experiences with him aboard the last airplane in U.S. airspace on 9/11. I then showed a few photos of me with the president and some shots of Air Force One, the Pentagon, and Capitol Hill.

Shifting gears, I explained how and why I made the transition from Navy commander to my current work as an evidential medium. I pressed a button on my remote control, and up popped a photo of my Susan in her Marine Corps sergeant's uniform. As was true in every presentation when Susan's photograph flashed on the screen, I had to fall back on military discipline to maintain my composure.

Susan's death at age 27 had been so unexpected. Married only seven months earlier, she was six months pregnant with her first child. I told the audience how she had been crossing the flight line at Marine Corps Air Station Cherry Point, North Carolina, reporting for duty. The skies over the hangar were clear, although dark storm clouds were fast approaching. A fellow Marine yelled at Susan from a window, telling her to hurry. She picked up her pace, but too late. Suddenly, a deafening crack of thunder exploded at the same instant a jagged bolt of lightning thrust down, claiming the life of Susan and her unborn baby.

Focused on Susan's sparkling, dark eyes on the screen, I missed what was happening in the front row of the audience. Upon hearing how I had lost my daughter, Mike and Beth had grabbed each other's arm. They knew nothing about me when they sat down to hear my presentation. Beth's ears had perked up when I reviewed my credible background, but when I described how Susan had passed, both she and Mike came instantly to the same realization: *This was why they had come.* It wasn't for the other speakers. It was for me. Why? Because their son, Wolf, had also been killed by lightning.

I knew nothing of this when Mike approached me after my talk. I wasn't present earlier when Maureen Hancock had singled out him and Beth in front of the cameras. He would have looked no different than the other attendees waiting in line for me to sign a book, except for two things. He was wearing a black T-Shirt with the image of a gray wolf's face emblazoned across the front. And he was wearing a look of deep intensity that silently pleaded with me to listen to his story.

Mike introduced himself and told me that he had lost a son who went by the name of Wolf. My heart opened wide for this man who was so obviously grieving. When he said, "He was struck by lightning," I did a double-take. I knew from my research after Susan's death that thousands of people are killed by lightning strikes each year, but Mike was the only parent I had ever met whose child had suffered that same fate.

"How can I help you?" I asked, suddenly unaware of anyone else in the area.

"My son knew he was going to die," Mike replied in a tone that defied disbelief. "How is that *possible?*"

My eyes locked on his as I answered him with three short words: "The soul knows."

This I knew because I had received a visit from Susan's spirit two days before she passed. In the non-physical dimension, time does not unfold linearly as it does here in our physical world. At the soul-level, events that would happen two days hence were visible and knowable. At the human level of consciousness, Susan had no inkling that her time on Earth was coming to an end. She was fully focused on her husband and baby and her impending role as a mother.

I told Mike how Susan's soul came to me in a vivid dream that I can recall today as clearly as I had the night it occurred. Spirit visits of this kind are remarkable because they stay with you and do not fade away in wispy tendrils when trying to remember them. In the dream, Susan walked up to me at a party and smiled. Standing face to face she assured me that she and the baby were fine. In the days following her death, I found great solace in this enduring message of reassurance.

"But this wasn't a dream," Mike said, referring to his son's premonition. "He knew how he was going to die and he knew exactly when and where it was going to happen. He even drew a picture of it!"

Now I was truly intrigued. For someone who insists on evidence, I concede that a visit in a dream will always be debatable. If Wolf left behind physical evidence foretelling his own death, this would bring a whole new level of credibility to soul communication. I needed to hear the details.

Mike launched into his story. Had I heard the actual howl of a wolf as Mike spoke with me there in that conference room, the hair on my arms would not have stood more on end. Mike was right. His son knew. The evidence he left behind is irrefutable.

CHAPTER TWO

The Soul Knows

For my husband and me it was a phone call that marked *The Moment*. If one could truly turn back the hands of time, the phone call when we learned that Susan had been killed marked the point at which we would rewind the clock. For Mike and Beth, it was a knock at the door. Rewinding the clock of their lives would put the big hand somewhere between 2130 and 2145 on September 8th, 2010.

Mike answered the door. The two men standing under the porch light wore civilian clothes. The large sedan in the driveway behind them bore no special markings. One of the visitors identified himself as a Massachusetts state trooper; the other as a detective with the Plymouth police force. Mike could not imagine why they had come. His son lived in Plymouth, just twenty-four miles north of the family home in Mashpee on Cape Cod. But he had never had any trouble with the law. In fact, Mike had spent a pleasant afternoon with Wolf just the day before.

He led the men to the side of the house and invited them in through the door. Beth joined them at the table in the sunroom.

"We need to ask you some questions," the detective said. "Do you have a son who lives in Plymouth?"

Mike glanced at Beth. "Yes, I do," he confirmed.

Had he been more intuitive, he would have felt a sense of dread. Instead, he suspected nothing amiss until the detective uttered the next sentence. That, according to Mike, was when Hell arrived.

"I'm sorry to tell you this, sir," the man said, pausing to take a breath. "We found his body."

The words *"We found his body,"* bypassed Mike's brain and slammed into his chest. He crumpled onto the table, feeling as if his heart had been ripped out.

They explained that a couple from North Carolina had come across a lifeless young man lying under a tree. "I'm so sorry," he said as Mike and Beth broke out in sobs.

They wanted desperately to believe that what they were hearing was a mistake. The detective dashed their hopes when he looked at Mike and said, "Now we know for sure that he's your son. He looks just like you."

Somehow Beth found her voice and asked what happened.

They learned that the couple from North Carolina had been walking around Burial Hill. The cemetery was a frequent stop for tourists because it held the remains of some of the original passengers on the *Mayflower*. The marker described it as historic and sacred ground. With its hilltop view of peaceful Plymouth Harbor, it was one of their son's favorite places to write, draw, and meditate.

"We don't have all the details at this point," the detective said, "but we think he may have been climbing a tree and fell and broke his neck. It appears this happened between half past five and six o'clock this evening."

Mike put his face in his hands. He had just seen Wolf. How could he be gone? The story didn't make sense. Why would Wolf climb a tree? He was twenty-nine—too old to be climbing trees and far too young to die.

"We're very sorry," the trooper repeated. "This is the worst part of our job, informing parents."

The detective nodded his head in agreement. "We assure you that between our two departments we're using every available resource to find out what happened."

Mike asked them to call Wolf's biological mother. He and Beth then listened to the details a second time, but their brains still wouldn't allow in the truth. After the policemen left, Mike repeated the dire news three times in phone calls to each of Wolf's uncles. The repetition did little to usher in reality. It only cast him further into an abyss.

Sleep eluded him and Beth that night. The thought of Wolf lying hurt and alone on the ground was more than their hearts and minds could bear. The concept of never seeing their son again was unthinkable.

At the crack of dawn they got in their car and drove to Plymouth. The police had taken Wolf's body to the medical examiner's office and were still conducting their investigation. Mike and Beth did not have a key to his apartment, but it didn't matter. They simply needed to be near their son, to walk in his footsteps and start looking for answers.

Forty-eight hours earlier Mike had driven the same route, compelled for some unknown reason to take the day off and spend time with Wolf. Had he known it would be the last time he would see his son, he would have said or done a thousand things differently. Had he known it was their last goodbye, he never would have left.

They drove directly to Burial Hill. The detective had told them that Wolf was found under a tree, but he hadn't indicated which one. There were many trees to choose from amid the park-like property. As they pulled into the parking lot and headed up a set of stone steps, they spotted a pair of latex gloves on the path. Farther ahead a second pair lay near a gnarled tree, as if to mark their way along the trail. Judging by the width of that big old beech tree, it had likely witnessed every interment in the cemetery since the earliest days of the Pilgrims.

Just a few feet from its thick roots lay a small brown hat embroidered with distinctive black skulls. Mike's knees threatened to buckle. The gloves were cold and impersonal, but the hat shouted out Wolf's name. How many times had he seen his son wear that hat?

He raised his eyes from the ground to the branches above, trying to imagine what this tree had seen. He reached out a hand and pressed it against this living, breathing witness to his son's final breaths.

Mike and Beth gazed at the deserted grounds. Word would soon spread about Wolf's tragic passing. Mike wanted to leave a simple but majestic tribute at the spot where his son had left the Earth. They returned to their car and drove to a nearby flower shop. Mike had come up with the idea to buy two red roses—one from him and one from his step-mother. If the florist wondered why the couple who bought the two roses was crying, she kept her questions to herself.

They returned to the cemetery and solemnly stuck the roses in the ground at the base of the tree. The green plastic water tube on each stem helped the two flowers to stand tall, just as six-foot-three-inch Wolf had stood.

Unable to enter Wolf's apartment until the police completed their investigation, Mike and Beth wandered the streets of downtown Plymouth visiting his favorite haunts. They stopped at The Blue Blinds Café, a popular bakery on North Street featuring a wide porch and traditional colonial furnishings. Wolf had often spoken of how he and the locals at the other tables had engaged in open discussions while enjoying fresh pastries and artisan breads.

Finding no one familiar at Blue Blinds, they walked on to the Laughing Moon gift shop at the corner of North and Main. The storekeeper, Nancy, was visibly shocked to hear the news. She informed Mike and Beth that Wolf had visited the store the day before. She was busy helping a customer and didn't have time to speak with him. When she returned to the counter, she saw that he had left a heart-shaped stone for her. He had a knack for finding these special stones and often gave them as gifts.

Later in the afternoon Mike's cell phone rang. The Plymouth detective who had delivered the horrible news the night before identified himself. This time he relayed information that brought both shock and relief: The medical examiner had determined that Wolf had not been killed as a result of an accident, negligence, or foul play. He had been struck by lightning and had died instantly. The shock came from the thought of such a random and violent death. The relief came from knowing that he hadn't laid on the ground in agony and suffered alone.

With the investigation closed, the detective informed Mike and Beth that they were free to pick up Wolf's personal effects. These included his wallet and the key to his apartment. While at the police station, they received a copy of the police report in which the detective mentioned the sudden change in weather. He later informed Mike and Beth that the storm that took Wolf's life was surprisingly localized. When the detective had noticed the intensity of the dark clouds he had called his wife at their home north of town to tell her to close the windows.

"What are you talking about?" his wife had replied. "It's beautiful here!"

Now that they had the key to Wolf's apartment, Mike and Beth drove to the modest complex of two-story brick buildings that Wolf called home. With no purpose other than to feel Wolf's presence, they entered the silent space.

Any visitor unfamiliar with Wolf's unusual décor would do a double-take at first glance. Wolf had covered nearly every inch of the walls and ceiling with a chaotic collage of posters, photographs, and his own drawings and writings. The shock effect came from the dissonant juxtaposition of bright colors, the clash of dark and light, and the unusual subject matter, much of which had an other-worldy, gothic feel.

In spite of the apparent chaos, Wolf had placed his artwork with great care, aligning each piece vertically and horizontally. Tacks in every corner held the papers firmly in place. A small plastic tub with extra tacks sat on the dining room table. Seeing them, Mike recalled words Wolf had written one year earlier to explain what the collection meant to him:

> *It started out with all these*
> *Empty white walls, then with*
> *A few pictures in the bedroom.*
>
> *I'd had this vision or dream:*
> *Cover all my walls*
> *With all kinds of pictures to make a*
> *New light in the eyes of an artist.*

I never dreamed it would be this
Hard to gather all that I would need.
Thousands upon thousands of tacks
Instead of using tape.

Most of the pictures hold
Some kind of memories
Of what I was doing
Or where I was, or perhaps
What a friend was going through.

Good or bad, light or dark
Makes no difference
I have created on my own
A world of art

That completely surrounds me
On every level.
I would never trade my home
For a million places on the globe.

Mike sank onto one of two couches in the living room. Wolf had painted their white cushions with dark cartoon-like figures, including a gray wolf's face with large yellow eyes. A row of hand-drawn rune symbols decorated the skirt of one couch, giving it the appearance of a string of ancient hieroglyphics.

Mike's eyes scanned the living room and dining room. As strange as the art might appear to others, he had grown accustomed to his son's eclectic taste. He had visited Wolf every two to three weeks, and every time he did, he walked around as if in a museum, studying the walls in each room to see what was new. There was always something different because Wolf tended to rearrange the entire collection every three months.

Now, in light of what happened, Mike puzzled over a pronouncement Wolf had made to him a month earlier. "I'm done moving everything," Wolf had said. Mike hadn't bothered to ask why.

"Do you notice something strange?" Beth asked from the entrance to the kitchen.

"Yeah," Mike said, following her gaze. "It's way too neat."

Usually when they came to visit, the place looked as if it had been hit by an earthquake. Today, the floors and surfaces were clear of clutter. Wolf's belongings were placed neatly on the shelves. No food was left on the kitchen counters; no dirty dishes filled the sink. Indeed, it looked as if Wolf had gone to great pains to leave everything in perfect order.

While Mike remained on the couch distraught and trying to make sense of everything, Beth wandered to the bedroom where she found the bed neatly made. No clothes littered the floor. Just as in the front rooms, not a single item was out of place. She crossed the hall towards what she called "the nature room." While every other room contained a mixture of art and writing, the walls and ceiling in this sanctuary where Wolf meditated held only artwork, predominantly photographs of exotic fish, animals, birds and lush landscapes.

The moment she entered the room, an 8 ½" by 11" piece of white paper caught her eye. It stood out because it was the only paper on the walls crafted by Wolf's hand. She stepped closer and looked up, certain that she had never seen this piece before. A large drawing in the shape of a human eye dominated much of the page. In the center of the eye where the cornea would be, he had drawn a yin yang symbol. The rest of the eye was filled with squiggly lines typical of Wolf's art. Beth paid the picture scant attention, drawn instead to the poem flanking it. Time seemed to slow as the significance of Wolf's words became clear.

"Mike!" she shouted. "You have to come and see this."

Responding to the urgency in her voice, Mike was quickly at her side. She pointed up at the poem tacked just below the edge of the ceiling. Together they read what appeared to be Wolf's last creative effort, written only days before he would be struck and killed by lightning:

> *Spirit of Great Healer*
> *Awaken from within this heart.*
> *Peace and tranquility flow like water.*
> *The time has come*
> *To allow the light of nature*
> *To free my soul.*

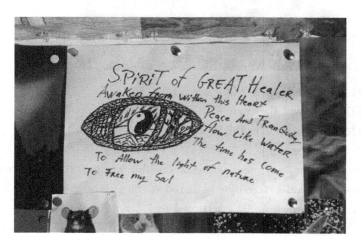

They stared at each other, dumbfounded. At a loss for words, Mike looked around the room. He noticed that the chair in which Wolf sat to meditate had been placed so that it directly faced the poem. As Mike's gaze focused on the wall behind the chair, he froze.

"My God."

Beth followed his gaze and caught her breath. There amid the many nature photographs was yet another foreign object. They recognized it immediately. It was the remains of one of Wolf's T-Shirts. They had photographs of Wolf in that shirt. In fact, Wolf had been wearing it the last time Mike saw him, just two days earlier.

For some reason Wolf had cut out the front of the shirt and tacked it to the wall. The rectangular black cloth now showcased its striking design: a jagged, white bolt of lightning that squarely faced Wolf's prophetic poem.

"How did he know?" Mike gasped.

"I don't know." Beth said softly.

"How do you explain this?"

"I can't."

They left the apartment without touching a thing. As far as they were concerned, the walls were now as sacred as the ground at Burial Hill. They drove home to Mashpee, but returned to Plymouth every day for the next few days. They told everyone who knew and loved Wolf what had happened. Over time a small memorial sprang up at the base of the tree consisting of candles, a few cans of Wolf's favorite soft drinks, a couple of his drawings, and some flowers. But none was as majestic as the two red roses Mike and Beth had placed there during their initial visit.

They continued to drop in at Wolf's favorite places, talking to his friends and piecing together the events of his final hours. Quite a few people remembered how Wolf had been hanging out with them at the Blue Blinds when he abruptly got up and announced, "I have to go now."

He loped off in the direction of his apartment, running into his friend Jim along the way. As far as Mike and Beth could determine, Jim was the last person to see Wolf alive. Jim told them that he assumed Wolf was going home, but the beech tree where he was found was not along the route to Wolf's apartment. It was as if he had gone to the cemetery on purpose.

Those who had been in the downtown area remembered the highly localized storm. They recalled how quickly it came up, seemingly out of nowhere. Several people reported hearing a single, deafening crack of thunder.

As the end of September approached, Mike and Beth were faced with cleaning out Wolf's apartment. They didn't want to touch the walls. Such an act represented a finality they were not yet ready to accept, but it made no sense to renew the lease. With no choice but to disassemble the inimitable collage, Mike hired a professional photographer to preserve it on film. They asked him to take pictures of every room from every angle. After that, Mike planned to collect all of Wolf's original drawings and poetry and keep them safe at home in Mashpee.

Knowing that their time in Wolf's apartment was limited, Mike and Beth wandered through the familiar rooms, once again perusing the artwork. They ended up in the nature room, staring at Wolf's final poem which was now forever inscribed on their hearts.

The time has come to allow the light of nature to free my soul …

So many other things in Wolf's final hours seemed to confirm that he had somehow known he was going to die. He had told his father he was finished moving his art around. He had cut the lightning bolt out of a favorite T-Shirt and tacked it to the wall across from a poem that presaged the exact manner of his death. He had tidied up his apartment as if he knew he wasn't coming back. And he had told his friends moments before the fatal storm, "I have to go now."

Each strand in this web of strange happenings would be confounding on its own. Woven together, they created a mystical tapestry that was beyond Mike and Beth's ability to comprehend.

Beth noticed the picture first. Afterwards, they would wonder how they missed it earlier. Something about the hand-drawn eye on that final poem suddenly caught her attention. She had focused on the yin-yang symbol at the center each time she had looked at it before. The yin-yang symbol was a common theme in Wolf's artwork. This time, however, she looked to the right of the symbol and inhaled sharply.

"Mike," she said, "I don't believe this."

He looked to where she was pointing and gasped. What had been in clear sight all this time in the eye drawn by Wolf suddenly came into distinct focus. To the right of the yin-yang symbol, Wolf had drawn not just a series of squiggly lines. He had drawn a recognizable image, compellingly visible now to the inquiring minds of his parents. What they saw, to their utter stupefaction, was the distinct shape of a gnarly old beech tree. And there, at the base of its thick trunk, stood two, tall, majestic red roses.

CHAPTER THREE

Reality Shifts

When Mike approached me at the Soul Life conference, I didn't appreciate
how clearly Wolf had foreseen his destiny. There wasn't time for him to share
the whole story with me while we were standing in the auditorium. Several
months would pass before I would hear all of the details.

Having just delivered a presentation about connecting with higher consciousness, I reviewed with Mike the central point that the physical world
is not as solid as it appears. All that exists, including our bodies, can be
broken down into waves of energy. We tend to differentiate reality into two
dimensions: the physical and the non-physical. In actuality, All That Is is
one big, pulsating field. The space around us is not empty. It is teeming with
information-carrying waves of energy.

The challenge for most humans is that we are easily deceived by our
perceptions. The brain is not the source of our consciousness, but an instrument that interprets information sent to it from the physical senses. There is
a limit to the frequencies in the environment that the brain can detect. Thus,
we end up basing our beliefs on what is perceived through the brain's filters.
In one sense, this is a good thing. If we were able to detect the full range
of frequencies around us such as radio, television, and cell phone signals,
we would experience chaos. Unfortunately, these same filters also prevent
most people from detecting the finely tuned vibrations emanating around us,
including those from our loved ones no longer in physical form.

I reminded Mike that just because we cannot see or hear something
doesn't mean it doesn't exist. At a soul level, all of us are tuned in to the
higher frequencies of the non-physical world. We walk in two worlds at
once as spirit-beings temporarily existing in human form. The physical and
the non-physical dimensions are intimately interconnected. Signs of this

interconnection abound, but with our consciousness focused primarily on the physical, we tend to tune out what can often be subtle yet very meaningful signals. If Wolf knew details about his own death, his soul was picking up information that existed at a level beyond a human's ability to comprehend.

Mike thanked me for that information. I sensed a mix of sadness and confusion in his energy as he walked away. I wasn't sure if my words had spoken to him.

I didn't see Mike again that day. The conference organizers kindly gave me a lift to my hotel, and I went to my room to rest. Had I stayed behind to await the shuttle, I might have witnessed Mike and Beth's discovery of a major sign from the other side. Unlike the subtle signals we had just discussed, this was an unmistakable gift from their son. Months later, when they shared the story with me, the magic of the moment remained fresh.

The shuttle from the conference to the hotel wasn't due to arrive for a while, so Mike and Beth had some free time on their hands. By unspoken agreement they began climbing the steps leading up a hill to the historic hospital built by Edgar Cayce in 1928. At the top they discovered a labyrinth forty feet in diameter. Together they watched as a lone woman slowly walked along the gray and tan bricks laid out in a circuitous path. With her eyes transfixed on the ground before her, the woman seemed oblivious to the presence of other people.

Beth made to continue on toward the hospital building. But Mike, his curiosity piqued, urged her to accompany him to the center of the over-sized maze. He knew from conference literature that the area was designed to encourage a meditative state, but when he saw the design at the heart of the labyrinth, his mind went on high alert. "Beth," he called softly, "Do you recognize this?"

She looked to where he was pointing. Recognition took only a moment. "It's just like the picture Wolf drew," she exclaimed. Together they stared in amazement at the design.

Large bricks had been cut and crafted to create a clearly-defined yin-yang symbol. More colorful than the traditional black and white design, a sky blue tear drop curved into an opposing navy blue twin to form a full circle. Where each of the two halves would normally contain a small dot of the opposite color, the labyrinth's designer had taken some creative license.

Gray and white bricks fit like pieces of a puzzle to depict a large dolphin in each half of the symbol. The two dolphins faced each other head to tail as if frolicking in the blue-brick water.

Mike and Beth shook their heads in wonder. Some years earlier Wolf had gone through a "dolphin stage." He often drew these graceful, happy mammals and tacked his drawings on the walls of his apartment. One drawing had been his favorite. It depicted a patterned field of small circles surrounding a non-traditional yin-yang symbol. Instead of the traditional black and white motif, he colored one half blue and the other orange. Just like the yin-yang design on the grounds of the A.R.E., each teardrop shape contained one large dolphin facing the other as if they were frolicking together.

Mike and Beth knew that Wolf had never been to the A.R.E. He had no connection with the organization. Neither of them could remember exactly how long ago Wolf had drawn his picture, but they were sure it had to be at least twenty years. He therefore could have seen this image on the Internet and copied it. Besides, Mike later told me, most of Wolf's art was original. He rarely copied anything.

They stood speechless, contemplating the significance of encountering one of Wolf's iconic drawings at the conference site. The unexpected discovery of the labyrinth confirmed what they realized earlier: They were in the right place at the right time. Had their shuttle not turned in on 67th Avenue at that moment to pick them up, they might have stayed longer and walked the path of the labyrinth. It would have been a new experience, but the whole weekend was full of firsts.

"Somber" is the word I would use to describe Beth's demeanor whenever I saw her that weekend. She caught my eye more than any other guest at the conference. Most of those in attendance exuded an air of either peace and contentment, or happiness and excitement. Beth stood out as one who sat silently with a furrowed brow, as though in contemplation of something life-defining.

Until I saw her with the man in the wolf T-Shirt I didn't realize that she and Mike were a couple. I was not present when they spoke with Maureen Hancock on camera. Once I put them together, I wondered if her somber air might be caused by a lingering sense of grief. She later explained that while she still mourned Wolf, she spent most of her time at the conference in a state of deep introspection. She had traveled to Virginia with her baggage full of archaic beliefs. Ever the dogmatic scientist, she had not easily accepted what those around her seemed to take on faith.

Something clicked for Beth at that conference. She stepped through the door into a new world. Much of what the presenters shared provided a framework with which to understand the events surrounding Wolf's death. The thought that ran repeatedly through her head during the resulting periods of introspection was, *What have I been missing?*

On the final morning of the conference I saw Mike and Beth enter the hotel restaurant. I was enjoying breakfast with my friend Elizabeth and a conference guest we had met in the elevator. The woman was in the middle of sharing a story when Mike and Beth caught my eye. The same force that repeatedly drew them into my awareness now propelled me to excuse myself and go to them. "I'll be right back," I said, placing my fork down on the table. Elizabeth gave me a puzzled look, but I didn't stop to explain.

A niggling voice of left-brain reasoning told me that what I was about to do made no sense. I already had a backlog of more than two hundred people waiting patiently for me to give them a reading and the list wasn't getting any shorter. My first obligation was to them, that voice insisted.

Then the right side of my brain kicked in as someone up above pulled rank.

Waiting list be damned. I was supposed to give them a reading as soon as possible.

CHAPTER FOUR

Unexpected Visitor

While I presented at the Soul Life conference in Virginia Beach, my husband Ty was holding down the fort, so to speak, in Fort Collins, Colorado. Three weeks earlier we had left our central Florida home on a ten thousand mile speaking tour across the United States and Canada. Our two longhaired miniature dachshunds, Rudy and Gretchen, loved traveling with us in our forty-foot coach. Each place we stopped offered new sights and scents for the pups. Fort Collins offered Ty a chance to do some hiking, biking, and fishing while I was back on the East Coast.

Ty takes a lot of good-natured ribbing about his tendency to fish and not catch anything. That he actually caught a good-sized trout while I was away (not to mention two really big ones that conveniently got away) received top billing that weekend on his popular travel blog, *Life As Ty Sees It*. He was only too pleased to inform his followers that his glorious achievement came about after he exchanged a bronze lure shaped like a spoon for a shiny one replete with silver spinners.

The day after my return I learned exactly how that poor trout must have felt. Foolishly, I allowed myself to be lured into a nearby RV dealership by a row of shiny new coaches parked in full view of the highway near our campground. The salesman must have recognized a couple of live ones he could reel in when we drove onto the lot—because we drove out of it with a brand new 42-footer. Ty merely shook his head. I may be the psychic one in our marriage, but he knew full well that we were doomed from the moment I said, "Let's just take a look."

We enjoyed breaking in our new home on wheels as we headed west across the Rockies. My first turn at driving our Greyhound-sized coach found us cresting the eleven-thousand-foot Eisenhower Pass. I discovered that when I reminded myself to relax and breathe, I could enjoy the majestic view through the coach's wrap-around windshield.

As June transitioned into July, we transitioned from the green forests of the higher elevations to the Mars-red desert of southern Utah. The stark beauty of the sandstone buttes in Monument Valley set the stage for the natural splendor we found hidden within the confines of northern Arizona's Antelope Canyon. Far more attuned to the vagaries of Nature than ever before, I savored the tangible difference in the "feel" of each place we visited. The compressed and downward flowing energy that left us hushed and awed inside the magical caverns stood in sharp contrast to the expansive uprush of vibration we experienced at the edge of the Grand Canyon's North Rim.

While spiritually uplifting, I was unable to do much work during this segment of our five-month trip. These remote areas in the Great Southwest, populated by people with long and deep traditions, offered few venues for my work as a medium. In addition, the lack of predictable cell phone or Internet signals prevented me from conducting readings via Skype or telephone.

I was able, however, to check email on almost a daily basis. As the weeks passed I found it surprising that I had not heard from Mike and Beth about a reading. I couldn't help thinking that if a medium had offered me the opportunity to connect with the spirit of my step-daughter Susan, I would have moved mountains to make it happen. With no contact information for Mike and Beth, I simply turned their decision over to Spirit.

Mid-July sent us seeking refuge from the fierce desert heat. Ty's carefully planned route took us to the cooler climes of the Pacific Northwest where we visited several old stomping grounds from my Navy days. Driving past the shore facility I commanded at Naval Station Bangor stirred memories that seemed a lifetime away from my current life's mission. I had lost contact with my staff, and wondered what they would think of their former skipper's forays into other dimensions.

Driving past the facility where I sent more than one wayward sailor to the brig conjured up an odd blend of emotions. On the one hand I felt immense pride and gratitude for the opportunity to serve my country, while on the other, immense gratitude for my new spiritual role that allowed me to simply follow my heart.

With two speaking engagements scheduled at churches in Canada, we motored on to Washington's Olympic Peninsula. I snapped multiple photos of Ty threading the coach onto a ferry headed across the Strait of Juan de Fuca to Victoria, British Columbia. A week later he repeated this daunting feat for the crossing to Vancouver where I received my first email from Mike since we had met in Virginia two months earlier.

He explained that he had sent several emails to me but had not heard back. He correctly sensed that the lack of response was due to a technological glitch and not to a lack of desire on my part to do a reading for him and Beth, which they still looked forward to very much.

In my reply I expressed my gratitude for his persistence and confirmed my own wish to connect them with their son as soon as possible. As much as I wanted to do the reading right away, Ty and I had not signed up for international cell phone or data service while in Canada. As fate would have it, we would be back in the United States the following week.

After all the difficulties I had had scheduling readings during the past two months, the timing of Mike's request turned out to be propitious. I had a speaking engagement coming up at a large church in Seattle. Ty had already reserved a campsite for several days at the military campground on the Army base at Fort Lewis south of Tacoma, Washington. I proposed a Saturday morning reading ten days hence via Skype. Mike replied that he and Beth would be sitting next to their computer on Saturday morning, July 20th.

Once I entered the appointed date and time on my calendar, I tried to dismiss it from my mind. With a reading for other people scheduled nearly each day while staying at Fort Lewis, I focused on keeping my thoughts in the present. Strangely, the primary spirit contact in each of the three readings preceding the one for Mike and Beth was a son who had passed in his twenties. Inevitably I wondered if the spirit world was somehow warming me up for Wolf's reading.

On Thursday morning, July 18th, I awoke at 5:45. Sunrise had officially clocked in fifteen minutes earlier, but in a campsite surrounded by tall fir and cedar trees it was still fairly dark outside. The coach's night shades blocked what feeble light was able to filter through the branches, leaving the bedroom as dark as a cave. I am by nature a morning person, but I had no desire that morning to leave our cozy bed. As I snuggled under the covers, an image of Mike and Beth flashed through my mind. I reminded myself that their reading was still two days away, and I turned over to go back to sleep.

Suddenly, a strong wave of vertigo had my head spinning. A few years earlier I would have been concerned by such an onslaught of inexplicable dizziness. Since then, I have learned to discern the higher vibrations of those in spirit, so I did not worry. Our bodies, I knew, are not actually solid. All physical matter studied under the finest microscopes reveals itself as a vibrating field of energy. At the start of a reading I ask those in spirit to blend their energy fields with mine. When they do so, I physically feel the shift. The higher the vibration of those who choose to communicate, the more lightheaded I become.

As I adjusted to what felt like a very powerful presence, I again saw the image of Mike and Beth and intuitively knew that my unexpected visitor was their son, Wolf. A shiver of excitement brought goose bumps to my arms. I could only recall two other instances when the spirit of someone's beloved had come to me unexpectedly. Both of those visits brought strong evidence with great clarity. Best of all, they represented the purest form of communication, with no feedback or clues from a family member in the room.

With Ty lying beside me in the bed, I sent a silent welcome to Wolf and rolled onto my side. I often receive guidance from my spirit guides at night and I sleep with a spiral notebook and pen on the nightstand. Now I pulled them close to record what Wolf had come to share.

The first thing he did was fill my head with images of hieroglyphics. I wrote, "*hieroglyphics ... symbols ... drawing.*"[1] Next he showed me a robed figure. I heard the word "*druid*" and wrote it down.

My readings are a combination of clairvoyance, clairaudience, and clairsentience. When the connection is good, I see, hear, and sense a mix of information that together paints a recognizable picture of those in spirit. Now I saw a necklace, I heard the word "*amulet*," and I sensed this meant that Wolf had worn some kind of man's necklace with an amulet.

To have an unexpected visit was a gift in itself, but I quickly grasped the uniqueness of this gift from the spirit world. I would often see a guitar or drum set in a reading if a loved one in spirit had once played in a band as a human. Or I would see them kicking a soccer ball if they played that popular

---

[1] All words in italics are verbatim, taken from the actual notes written during Wolf's unexpected visit.

sport. These were evidential, but common human interests. Mention of such things as hieroglyphics, symbols, druids, and amulets did not usually arise in sessions. The kind of evidence Wolf was sharing with me from the start of his visit was highly unusual and would be easy to validate.

Next he mentioned the number fourteen, but I had no sense of why it might be important. I wrote it down nonetheless, investing no time in puzzling over its meaning. Analyzing anything at that point would have shifted me out of the relaxed and receptive early-morning state of consciousness that had facilitated the visit. Worse, it might break the link.

He showed me hieroglyphics again, and then I heard, "*Mike.*"

"*Mike. Junior?*" I wrote with a question mark. It felt right, but I didn't know for certain. I realized that I had only heard Mike refer to his son by his nickname, Wolf.

He then showed me a hand hitting a stone with a chisel. "*Chiseling. Chiseling a message.*" Again the words made no sense, but I dutifully wrote them down.

I began to get a sense of Wolf's personality. "*Outdoorsy. Had great respect for nature. Shows me a fish mouth. Doesn't want to hurt it with the hook. Old, old soul,*" I wrote, then described how he showed me a figure who looked like an Indian standing on a cliff looking out at the distance.

The evidence flowed non-stop. If the scratching of my pen bothered Ty, he didn't let on. I feared that the initial motions of rolling over and adjusting the pad of paper had awakened him, but he remained silent. He knew that when I wrote in the dark I was usually receiving some kind of communication that required my full concentration.

I blindly guided my pen as I had learned to do, allowing my fingers to feel for the edge of the page. After each piece of information I methodically moved the tip of my pen a half inch down the page to avoid writing over anything.

Not happy in school socially
More of a loner, but very, very close to you
Watches over you like a hawk

He made me go back and underline the word "*hawk*" as if to emphasize its significance. Continuing with the bird theme, I wrote "*soaring,*" and then he showed me a bird hitting a window. That imagery came with the distinct feeling that Mike and Beth would recall a significant incident when a bird flew into a window.

It is surprising how loud a single sheet of paper can crackle when one is trying to be quiet. I winced each time I had to turn a page, until I noticed that something had changed. The raspy sound and deep, slow rhythm of his breathing indicated that Ty had fallen back asleep. It seemed impossible that he could drift off while my pen scratched away only two feet from his ears. But then again, naval officers learn to sleep "catch as catch can" and Ty had served for years as caption of a destroyer. In any event, I was grateful for the extra time with Wolf.

As I focused on the connection, Wolf rewarded me with a crystal clear vision of a little red wagon. *"Radio Flyer,"* I wrote after *"red wagon."* There seemed to be something special about the Radio Flyer brand.

Next I heard *"Über-intelligent,"* and I wrote, *"Why über?"* Wolf's last name, Pasakarnis, did not sound German to me. This communication was followed by images of what looked like a mad scientist at work. I wrote, *"Experiments. Like science. Beakers. In garage experimenting."*

With such a clear blending of our two energy fields, I found it easy to sense what he had been like as a human. I sensed that he wanted everyone to love each other on a grand scale, as in all of humanity. He held up two fingers in a "V" to form the peace sign, and he pumped it twice for emphasis. He seemed to care deeply about how people treated each other. To me, he seemed wise well beyond his years in human form.

Again he spoke of *"rituals ... sacred rituals,"* and showed me a figure that looked like Merlin the Magician morphing into a teenage boy and then back to Merlin again.

There didn't seem to be much rhyme or reason to the string of details I was receiving. Wolf bounced from showing me another image of a native American in a desert to flashing me the number eighteen. I attributed the popcorn-style clues to the challenging nature of spirit communication. Those on the other side can only communicate by manipulating energy. As the receiver of their frequencies, all I can do is try to fine-tune my antenna.

The signal seemed a bit garbled as Wolf shared a series of words that made even less sense to me. The question marks I wrote in the dark spoke volumes. They made it clear that I had no idea what he was trying to say: *"Jammin ... pajamas? ... Jama Mama?????"*

Undeterred, we continued in his role of communicator and mine as scribe. Four more times I turned the page, filling a total of eight sheets of paper.

"Have Mike and Beth score this, like Gary," he directed.

His request referred to my work with Dr. Gary Schwartz, Ph.D, a scientist and professor at the University of Arizona who is a noted afterlife researcher. I had been communicating with Gary for the past year and had participated in exploratory investigations into the continuity of consciousness at the university's Laboratory for Advances in Consciousness and Health.

During his fifteen years of evaluating mediums, Gary had developed a rigid system of scoring the evidence that mediums claimed to have brought through from the other side. He had applied his system to some of my readings with results that made the "A student" in me proud. Wolf must have known that to get me and others to trust what he was sharing in this unexpected visit, he needed to establish his presence scientifically.

I didn't know how much time had passed since I first sensed Wolf's presence. The external world seemed to stop when my consciousness merged with those in the realm of no time and no space. All I knew is that he had given me a tremendous amount of information that would be easy to validate. I shifted from receptive mode to active and silently asked, "Do you still want to do the reading on Saturday?"

"Yes, do the reading anyway," he replied, *"so they can ask questions and talk to me."*

He again held up his fingers, this time to communicate *"I love you"* in sign language. I often hear this important message in a reading, but not always. If a family member had difficulty expressing their love while in human form, I may feel their love in my heart, but they won't say the words. I had no doubt from the way Wolf felt that he would have said, "I love you" to Mike and Beth. The fact that he showed it to me in sign language felt significant in addition to the message itself.

The other-worldly feeling that accompanied his presence began to fade, and I felt myself coming back to awareness of the room around me. I wrote one last phrase from him on my notepad before opening my eyes: *"More to follow on Saturday."*

The bedroom had brightened somewhat. I stared at the ceiling fan, watching the blades turn in a slow circle as my mind started processing the information Wolf had shared. As I always try to do, I had kept myself in the dark about the details of his life in anticipation of his reading. I knew nothing about him before this unexpected visit other than the fact that he had died after being struck by lightning. Now I had dozens of pieces of information that seemed impossible to tie together into a coherent whole.

With Ty still dozing, I took my notepad, slipped out of bed, and walked quietly to the front room where I turned on my laptop and typed up everything that had come through. Most of the words were surprisingly legible. I saved the file, then opened a blank email and attached the document. I also attached a separate file from my folder on Dr. Gary Schwartz that explained how to score individual elements of a reading. I then typed the body of the email:

Dear Mike and Beth,

I am sure that Wolf visited me this morning.

Attached is a transcript of the notes I wrote in the dark. I think it will be very helpful if you will score each of these items according to the other document attached. This was Wolf's idea to have you score it, as you will see when you read the notes.

Please reply before Saturday morning and let me know your overall impression of the visit, but do not tell me what was or wasn't accurate so that I go into Saturday with no preconceived ideas.

With much love,

Suzanne

I hit "send" and sat back. Asking for their impression was the kind of thing I do during a reading to let me know if I am receiving the information correctly. Does the information make sense to them? Is it generally accurate? If not, I try a different technique to tune in better. During Wolf's unexpected visit, I had not had the luxury of anyone's feedback.

I knew that Mike and Beth would review each item with me after their reading. For now I only wanted to determine how clearly I had perceived their son's communication. My request was a formality, really. I didn't need their confirmation. I looked forward to getting to know Wolf better on Saturday morning, because I knew for certain that we had already met.

CHAPTER FIVE

The Reading

"We were blown away."

Mike stated his opinion of Wolf's visit more succinctly now that we faced each other on our computer screens than when he emailed me the day before. Both he and Beth had followed my instructions to the letter. They both scored each line of the data I sent them for accuracy, but they had not yet shared it with me. Instead, they sent me separate emails in which they provided only their general impression of the visit.

"There was no doubt that it was him," Beth wrote, "with a few pretty powerful specific messages."

"Wow!" wrote Mike on Friday. " Wolf coming to you was a blessing and provided more proof of our continued existence. There is no other explanation for the accuracy of your notes other than Wolf was with you. I am so looking forward to talking with you and Wolf tomorrow, and I'm preparing questions. I can't wait to blow your mind explaining some of Wolf's notes."

"Tomorrow" had arrived, and thanks to the modern technology of Skype, we smiled at each other from a distance of three thousand miles. I had done enough sessions by phone and Skype to know that the accuracy of the evidence received in a long-distance reading can be every bit as high as one conducted in-person. Whether or not my client is present with me makes no difference. Their loved ones in spirit express themselves as formless waves of consciousness. Their "signal" vibrates everywhere at once. Their world is not some far-off place; it is intertwined with our own world at a different frequency.

I shifted my chair and reached to the left to turn on an extra light. I often make gestures during a reading that show exactly what I am sensing before I verbalize it. I wanted to make sure Mike and Beth could see me clearly on the video. Now that I knew for certain that the presence I had felt two days earlier was Wolf, I was confident that we would reconnect.

"Okay," I said to Mike and Beth, "If you were here in person, I'd take your hands to say my opening prayer." I smiled and held out my hands toward the screen. "For now, just pretend I'm holding them."

My prayers tend to be somewhat unconventional. Having grown up with no formalized religion, I prefer prayers that come straight from the heart. Now I thanked God and my team of helpers on the other side for the opportunity to show Mike and Beth that their son was still very much with them. I asked for help in surrendering my human persona to become the clearest possible channel for whatever information Wolf wanted to share. I promised to do my best to relax and to fill the room with love, and I gave thanks for the best possible experience for all concerned.

I opened my eyes, uncurled my closed fists, and picked up the small digital tape recorder lying beside the computer. "I'll start recording now," I said as I pressed the red button, " and we'll see what we get."

I set the recorder next to the computer, sat back, and closed my eyes.

 "*I surrender*," I said silently as I took a deep breath. I slowly exhaled and shifted my awareness away from my body. I mentally invited Wolf to step into my energy field and blend his consciousness with mine. Within seconds I felt the room begin to swirl.

"Okay. Here we go. Whoa." I opened my eyes to steady myself and shook my head. "Phew! Okay, I feel the presence. The very f-f-f-first thing ..."

I tried to tell Mike and Beth what I was sensing, but the words came out in a stutter. I explained that the energy was very high, causing my hands to shake and my heart to skip a few beats. My heart often palpitates in a reading when the person on the other side had some kind of heart issue. I realized that the lightning strike may have affected Wolf's heart.

"*Go ahead and talk*," I said aloud to Wolf, confident that the presence I felt was Mike and Beth's son. "*What do you want to say?*"

I listened with as much concentration as I could muster. When I hear words and phrases in a reading, they sound no different than my own thoughts. This can make it difficult to discern if what I'm hearing is com-ing from my own mind or from the consciousness of a visiting spirit. When

I hear things that I could not have known or that I would not normally assume, I know it is coming from outside my own mind.

Wolf replied that he had come to me the other morning, but that he came to his father every night in his dreams. I passed this on to Mike and Beth, and then heard what sounded like the word "crackerjack." I felt as if I were swinging a bat. I asked Mike if Wolf had an interest in baseball.

"No," he replied.

I frowned and waved my hand as if fanning the air. The gesture helped me to clear the thought from my mind. I learned early on in my work as a medium not to let a few "no's" discourage me. I focused my attention back on Wolf.

"He's showing me writing, writing, writing, and I feel very introspective ... or drawing ... drawing. Writing and then drawing. Sketching."

"Yes," Mike said, leaning in.

"Phew. Lightheaded. *'It's far out there,'* he says. He's sketching things that don't make sense to other people."

"Exactly," Mike confirmed.

Only later when Mike shared a CD with hundreds of Wolf's pictures taken by a professional photographer would I come to understand how accurate this description was.

My head filled with more strange images. "I keep seeing pyramids, triangles, spirals, circles. He says, *'It was like going home to draw these things, like going home.'*"

I shook my head. The words didn't make sense on a rational level, but I knew he was referring to his spiritual home, not this earthly realm.

"He says he tried to explain this to people, and they just couldn't understand. They thought he had a fanciful imagination."

My heart palpitated a second time and I noticed my hands shaking. I didn't mind the extra energy. It generated an incredibly clear connection. "He's so strong!" I exclaimed, "But at the same time, he feels like he had a real gentle personality."

Describing what a soul's personality is like comes easily to me in a reading. When the blending of energy fields is good, as it was in this case with Wolf, it's as if I become that person. I feel as if I know him or her, because for a short while, I *am* that person. With our consciousness joined, we become *one*.

31

Sometimes those on the other side will share a particular character trait auditorially. I will hear a word like "patient," and I will then test that word against what I feel. Based on what I was hearing and feeling from Wolf, I could tell that he had been a gentle, kind, and very loving individual.

"Yes," Mike again confirmed.

I described what felt like a special connection with the animal kingdom. "He communicated better with animals than with people," I relayed, and for the first time Beth, the veterinarian, chimed in to agree.

The sensory impressions flowed non-stop with the kind of ease that I pray for in a reading. "I'm suddenly rocking," I said as I noticed myself swaying forward and backward in the chair. "And he's saying, *'Mention that,'* as though he would have rocked in the same way when in physical form."

I opened my eyes and looked at Mike and Beth. "This is the beauty of Skype, because you can s-s-s-see this. Boy, is he powerful! I love this energy."

Wolf's vibration was by far the highest I had felt in hundreds of readings from a family member on the other side. Mike would later tell me that medium Maureen Hancock had said the same thing when she gave them their reading. She claimed that Wolf felt like a little Buddha.

The full focus of that powerful energy suddenly shifted to my heart and I let out an involuntary moan. "I want to cry ... Strong emotion as he says, *'I had to go, Dad. I had to go, and I had to go like that,'*" meaning the lightning strike.

"Why?" Mike asked plaintively.

Wolf explained through me he had fulfilled his mission here on Earth, just as my step-daughter had. He and Susan had both come to leave their legacy, but apparently he wasn't sitting around idle now in the non-physical dimension.

"I still have work to do. I'm helping those on the other side who take their own lives."

"He's helping them to see what they'd done," I continued, amazed at these revelations. "'*I've now experienced life with them. I help the young ones.*'"

"Only the most spiritually developed souls would help people with that," I informed Mike and Beth.

"There's no proving this," I said as my logical mind momentarily kicked in, "but he's saying, *'You'll understand it some day.'* He experienced life here, and he knows the struggles we face on Earth. He can help those who take their own lives. He helps them adjust and grow spiritually."

"Okay, now let's get back to this life here," I said aloud to Wolf. *"Show me more about you."*

In response to my request, I saw a series of images with wheels: bicycles, skateboards, and wagon wheels. "I'm supposed to talk about that red wagon that he brought up the other day."

"He had bicycles," Mike said. "And I used to pull him around in a red wagon, but ..."

I shook my head. That wasn't it. Every little kid had a bicycle and a wagon. Drawings and symbols with circles spun before my eyes. Wolf was trying to tell us something about wheels, but none of us could determine what or why.

"He's talking to me about sacred geometry now," I relayed, "because at the soul level those shapes spoke to him."

My attention was drawn to my right hand. "Why am I doing this with my pen?" I asked aloud. "It's making a circle. The circle is the symbol of oneness and unity, and I have a sense that at a soul level he understands that this is why we're here and what this life is all about. He really is 'up there.' He really is advanced at a soul level."

Mike and Beth said very little. They seemed stunned by the intensity of our exchange and the information being revealed.

I then saw a series of images that took me to the desert, then on to Arizona and the Grand Canyon, where Wolf seemed to have had a sacred experience. Mike informed me that he and Beth had scattered some of Wolf's ashes in the Grand Canyon. Wolf then showed me a lightning bolt, the cause of his death. He followed this image with a string of details, including some that Mike and Beth could not confirm. I pushed those aside and asked for more clarity.

Wolf complied by showing me a circle in the ground. I recognized what I was seeing, but I couldn't find the word. "This is one of those things you walk in that looks like a maze on the ground. What is it called?"

Mike's body jerked. "At the A.R.E. conference we walked up to the hospital and they had a large maze in front."

"Labyrinth!" I said as the word popped into my mind. "Labyrinth! That's it!" Mike nodded enthusiastically.

"Excellent! He's showing me the labyrinth," I said, unaware that Wolf had just made reference to what had been an incredibly meaningful moment for Mike and Beth. They had not shared their discovery of the labyrinth with me prior to the reading, but the goose bumps breaking out on my arms confirmed that this bit of evidence held special importance to Wolf as well.

"He drew the two dolphins and the yin-yang symbol that are in the center of that labyrinth at the A.R.E." Beth said.

"Wow. *Good one!*" I said to Wolf. "*Give me some more.*"

Wolf flashed a number before my eyes. "Is the number twenty-four significant?"

Before Mike or Beth could respond, I saw a different image. "He shows me a birthday cake right now. Somebody has a birthday, and I don't count that as a hit unless it's right around two weeks from now."

"Two weeks from now is Beth's birthday," Mike said.

I laughed. "There we go!"

"And the 24th is my mother's birthday," he added.

"Okay! Very good. *Thank you for that one,*" I said to Wolf.

I then described seeing a target and hearing the word "bingo."

"I'm supposed to talk about that target," I continued. "I'm seeing archery symbols. Archery ... archery ... but a target. Does that make any sense?"

In the brief moment that I waited for Mike to respond, I experienced the same excited expectancy as if I were actually playing Bingo. The details Wolf was sharing were far from generic. Each time Mike or Beth responded with a meaningful explanation, I felt as if we had all won the jackpot.

"My brother is an archer," Mike said, "and he shoots all the time. He taught Mike how to shoot, and got him his bow and arrows."

The confirmation pleased me, but not so much as hearing Wolf referred to by his real name. "*So you were right about that the other day, too,*" I silently said to Wolf. He was, indeed, '*Mike Junior.*'

"He's so *here!*" I said, smiling. "That's great. *Okay. You're doing great, Wolf. Keep going.* He said, '*No, you're doing great.*'" I laughed. "*Okay, then let's do it together.*"

As is often the case, I couldn't help wondering how this unusual dialogue might sound to anyone who happened to drop in during the middle of a reading.

"He's saying, '*I had to go, Dad. It's all I signed up f-f-f-for ... now go out and change the world.*'" Wolf meant they were supposed to make something good come of his death. He reminded me of the dramatic way in which he left this world and stressed that people would listen to his messages because of it.

"The papers ..." I gave a shake of my head as the word spilled from my mouth in rapid fire. "Papers, papers, papers, papers ... You talked about the poems, but there are stacks of them. And a lot of them are loose leaf."

"Yes," said Mike and Beth in perfect unison.

"He's showing me that you've gathered them together. Oh! He says, *'Thanks for keeping them s-s-s-safe.'* There's something about that word 'safe.' They're in a special place, or something could have happened to them, but it didn't. Does that make sense?"

Mike and Beth exchanged a knowing look before Mike explained. "I took them all and I have them at my house. We had a photographer photograph his house, because every square inch of walls and ceilings were covered with his paintings, and drawings, and poetry. Every week he moved them from one place to another until about a week before it happened, and he said, 'I'm done moving them.'"

Again my arms erupted in goose bumps. I sent Wolf waves of gratitude for the spectacular way he was showing his parents that he was still with them.

"He says, *'S-s-s-some ...'*" I paused to again explain that my stuttering was from the continued high energy of Wolf's spirit. *"S-s-s-some people would have said that was crazy'*—to have those things on the walls—but he couldn't stop the flow, because he couldn't break the connection with the other dimension. *'It was just constant channeling,'* he says. He was *'tethered'*, he says, *'tethered'* to the other side. Do you get that?"

"Yes, absolutely."

I nodded, and then experienced a new sensation. "Why am I suddenly in a parachute? I'm strapped in, and I'm holding onto the straps." My hands grasped two imaginary straps across my chest.

"He drew some chains across his heart," Beth said.

"He drew posters with chains across his heart, like he was tied up," Mike explained.

"That's the image I have," I confirmed. "Did you see me go like that?" I repeated the motion of grabbing at the straps, grateful once again for the video connection courtesy of Skype.

"I'm asking him, *'What's with the parachute?'* and now he's showing me a hot air balloon, and there's something about this connection with the sky."

Mike furrowed his brow, and then told me that two years earlier he and Beth had gone up in some hot air balloons.

I shook my head. I never agreed to a client's interpretation just to get a "yes" if it didn't feel right. "He's telling me that's not why he's showing me the hot air balloons. He's trying to get through this constant connection he had with '*more than the Earth*' – so that's why I'm sensing the parachuting and the balloon images. He was '*in both ...*' That's it! '*In both worlds at once, all the time*' ... like he couldn't turn it off. It feels like he's trying to show me that his brain was wired differently than other people's."

"Yeah," Mike agreed.

"In fact, he shows me grades that are down here," I lower my hand toward the floor. "So, C's, D's, and F's."

Beth confirmed, "He couldn't keep up in normal schoolwork."

"Because he was wired differently," I repeated, pleased by the confirmation. "'*It was very busy in here*,' he says," and I pointed at my head as I saw Wolf doing in my mind's eye. "Very busy in his head."

"He always said that," Mike informed me.

I pumped a fist. I love it when those on the other side give me things their family can attribute directly to them. This, after all, is the whole point of evidential mediumship: to prove that consciousness survives the transition we call "death."

Now Wolf ran a video clip through my head that I had recently watched on Youtube. I excitedly shared with Mike and Beth that they were to google the subject of the film: a child prodigy who channeled the music he heard in his head and who produced symphonies rivaling those of Beethoven and Mozart.

"He wants you to watch that, so you underst-st-st-stand how the words and the symbols came to him. Okay?"

"Yes."

"There's a sense of him having difficulty holding down a job."

"Yes," Mike said. "He worked very infrequently."

"He says, '*I was not of this world!*'"

Then Wolf whispered a word in my ear that caused me to do a double-take, and I listened again to be sure. "He just said the word, 'schizophrenia.' Did somebody ever think that he had a mental illness?"

In unison Mike and Beth replied, "Yes."

36

Beth added, "He was diagnosed schizophrenic."

"Well, there's a good piece of evidence for you," I said, dumbfounded, as I tried to reconcile my human concept of mental illness with the presence of the most powerful spirit I had ever encountered in a reading. And then I had a burst of understanding, courtesy of Wolf.

"Wow. He's flashing before my head the presentation I just gave in Vancouver. A man in the audience raised his hand and said, 'Who's to say that people in mental institutions aren't just in another world?' and Wolf is nodding his head, nodding his head, meaning, '*Exactly*!' Do you get that?"

"Yep," Mike said.

We stared at each other across the miles for a long moment until Wolf interrupted.

"He says, '*Look how I passed. That's not an accident*,' Oh! Okay. He says that the dramatic way in which he passed will cause people to pay attention. '*This is to bring more empathy for those with mental illness. And it is an illness*,' he says, '*because there is a baseline of behavior in your world that is considered normal, and that is understandable, because you have to function*.'"

I was channeling his words now as they flowed, speaking directly for Wolf. "'*And you can see how I was in both worlds and unable to function on the normal baseline*.'"

Here he accompanied his concepts with a burst of emotion, and I emphasized his next words, "'*But there was nothing wrong with my heart*.'"

I thought of what incredibly loving and compassionate people Wolf and Susan were, and I shuddered. Both had been taken from this world by a powerful act of Nature.

"That was divine," I said, and then continued speaking for Wolf.

"'*And now I am higher than normal in this new world, and I am helping those who passed who also could not relate at the human level. I am helping them when they get to the other side*,' because he's operating higher than what's normal at the next level."

"Whoa." I blinked. "Did you get all that?"

"Yep," Mike said.

"It's amazing," said Beth.

I realized that my hands had been moving up and down the whole time Wolf was explaining the various levels of existence. "That's why we needed Skype. Did you see all the visuals he's giving me?"

"Crazy"

As Mike and Beth nodded, I turned my focus back to Wolf and continued.

"There are a lot of people who would call the stuff on the wall 'crazy' ... it just means 'not in the normal spectrum of v-v-v-vibrations.' He was getting b-b-b-bombarded with the higher vibrations, making it difficult to function in these very dense vibrations of the physical world. *'I feel sorry for you who have to live in this dense world. Just wait. You'll be lighter than air'* and he shows me the balloon again."

I suddenly clapped my hands in childlike joy. "There you go! *'On the other side you'll be lighter than air. I'm at home now. I'm at peace now.'*"

I nodded as I remembered Wolf talking earlier about his drawings reflecting his desire to go home.

"*'I'm going to come to you, Dad, like I came to her,'*" Wolf referred now to the unexpected visit he had paid me two days earlier. "*'I've been coming to you every night, Dad. Get your paper and pencil ready. I will give you a taste of what it was like for me to hear the voices. Write it down, Dad. It's me.'*"

Wolf told me to show Mike how to write in the dark. I held up the pad of paper and the pen that lay beside the computer and quickly shared my method.

"All right," I said as I finished the lesson. "And my heart just goes 'phew' with the love for you." I put a hand to my chest and fanned it outward. I then cocked my head to the side as Wolf shared a sentence that he wanted to make sure I got word for word.

"He says, *'I had a funny way of showing it.'* I don't understand that, but he loved you immensely. I don't know if he means that literally about having a funny way of showing you his love."

Mike beamed. "Every time we left each other, we gave each other this symbol." He held up his fingers in the American sign language symbol for "I love you."

I felt a burst of joy as I remembered Wolf showing me that same symbol with his fingers in his unexpected visit.

"Yeah! It felt like it was a funny way of actually showing it, so that's perfect. Now he says, *'That's what I meant!'* Okay, I hear you!" I said aloud to Wolf, laughing at his insistence.

I sat back and allowed the rush of love which enveloped me now to flow through to Mike and Beth. This was the payoff for having asked them not to give me any feedback from Wolf's visit two days earlier. I had no idea at the time if the "I love you" sign he showed me in those early morning hours held any significance or not. Clearly, that symbol was critically important.

"That's a good way to wrap it up," I heard from Wolf.

A good way, indeed, I thought, pleased beyond words at the outcome of the reading. As a grand finale, he had gotten me to talk about the very symbol he and his father used each time they said goodbye to each other, and he had done so with perfect timing as he brought this very special visit to a close. In doing so, Wolf succeeded in convincing his parents that he had never really left them.

My heart rate and breathing began to return to normal as I felt Wolf's consciousness withdraw from my energy field. He put three final words in my head, which I relayed to Mike and Beth.

"I'll be around," he says."

His message would prove to be far more prophetic than any of us could possibly have realized.

CHAPTER SIX

Validation

Connecting with loved ones who have passed requires suppressing the left-brain's tendency to analyze and question every detail. The best results come when a medium has trust in the process and focuses on feeling rather than thinking. This potent combination of trust and feeling allows the incoming information to bypass the brain's barriers and go straight to the heart. The more I'm able to set my doubts aside in a session, the better the connection.

I had no doubt after sitting with Mike and Beth that Wolf had communicated with us. That didn't make me any less eager to gather feedback immediately after their reading. I felt like a quarterback preparing to study the replays of a winning game. My left brain could hardly wait to analyze every detail. I looked forward to reviewing the highlights, but I also wanted to learn from any information that hadn't come through clearly.

Now, as Mike, Beth, and I compared impressions of Wolf's visit, I felt like an excited teenager. Words like "awesome" and "amazing" didn't seem to do justice to the sacred experience of receiving such clear communication from across the veil. I picked up the notes I'd scribbled while connected with their son and asked about those that I had highlighted.

"So he did a lot of writing and drawing" I observed, "including the hieroglyphics and symbols he showed me two days ago?"

Mike nodded. "He had hundreds of papers," he said. "They covered his walls and ceiling. I have them all safe at home now, just like you said. Wait until we send you some of the photographs of his apartment."

"The hieroglyphics were rune symbols," Beth commented. "He drew them a lot."

I nodded in turn. I knew that people had been using stones with symbols on them as divination tools since ancient times. However, I had never seen a set of runes or known anyone who used them.

This triggered another memory from his unexpected visit. "Wolf talked about rituals, and he showed me robed figures. Was he into that sort of thing?"

"Yes," Mike confirmed. "That, and anything to do with nature, just like you said."

"He explored a variety of world religions," Beth added.

As I scanned my notes, my eyes fell on the words *"red wagon."* I had starred this item after remembering that Wolf brought up a Radio Flyer wagon in his previous visit. During the reading, Mike and Beth couldn't remember any specific memories pertaining to a wagon. I asked them to think again about why it might be important.

"Nothing comes to mind," Mike said, "but come to think of it, Maureen Hancock also mentioned a Radio Flyer."

I blinked in surprise. If Wolf had shown the wagon to Maureen and he then showed it twice to me, there had to be a reason. I hoped this was simply a case of psychic amnesia. In my experience, clients often blank out a specific memory during a reading, only to receive a flash of insight later. Until that light bulb turned on for Mike and Beth, I could only wonder what Wolf was trying to tell us.

I glanced down at my notepad. I had circled the words *"in two worlds at once."*

"Do you understand what Wolf told us about why he didn't fit in here and what he meant by his desire to 'go home'?"

"What you said made a lot of sense," Beth said, but her voice lacked conviction.

They both seemed to be struggling with the concepts Wolf had brought to light. Because he provided such clear evidence about himself, I felt sufficiently confident to elaborate on his behalf.

"I think he must have always known at some level that there was another place where he fit in better. His soul knew that the greater reality was his real home, and he came back to let you know he's there now."

Mike slowly let out a breath. "It's just really hard to understand what it must have been like for him. This is all new to us."

I reminded Mike of what we talked about at the Soul Life conference: that all of us are at once both human beings and spirit beings. Most people are so fully focused on the physical experience that they become completely disconnected from the spirit side of their dual nature. I had spent most of my life in that state of unawareness that keeps us from knowing who we really are. I explained that like Wolf, I was now conscious of walking in both worlds at the same time. I connect regularly and intentionally with those on the other side. The big difference between Wolf and me was that I can turn off their voices at will.

I shook my head in wonder. "The things he told us put mental illness in a whole new light."

"It's a lot to think about," Mike said gently.

I asked him to elaborate on the extent of Wolf's challenges. Mike assured me that everything I sensed about his son's good nature was accurate. Wolf never caused harm to any soul, and they couldn't imagine him doing so. He expressed his inner turmoil only through his drawings and writing, which he admitted were often dark. Wolf truly did want peace on a grand scale. They had pictures of him making the peace sign, just as he'd shown me in his visit.

I reminded Mike and Beth how Wolf had stressed that there was nothing wrong with his heart.

"That's a fact," Mike said, nodding his head. "You should have seen the line of people waiting to get in when we had the wake for him in Plymouth. About four hundred people showed up. Four hundred! We had no idea he touched so many lives with his kindness."

I checked my watch and saw that we had been Skyping for nearly an hour and a half. I needed to wrap things up.

"Have you had a chance to score the evidence from Wolf's visit the other morning?" I asked.

"Yes," Beth responded, "and we sent our scores to Gary like you asked."

"Like *Wolf* asked," I corrected her with a smile.

They confirmed that per Professor Schwartz's instructions, they also provided one sentence after every item explaining the reason for the rating they had assigned it. This extra step ensured that they gave serious thought and attention to the task.

I thanked them for the time it must have taken to painstakingly go over each of the fifty-eight items.

"There's one more favor I need to ask," I said with a wince, aware that I was about to again impose on them.

"Gary likes to show that the results are not simply random chance. He'd like you to think of someone to serve as a 'control.' This should be a male relative who is about the same age as Wolf was when he passed."

Mike and Beth looked at each other, and I could see their minds working. "There's a cousin ..."

"Good. Then I want you to please go back over the list again and score it using the same method you did for Wolf. This time, though, imagine that the visitor I sensed on the other side was this cousin. Ask yourself, 'Did this cousin draw a lot? Did he do creative writing? Is there anything with hieroglyphics or symbols that pertain to him? Did he perform any special rituals?'"

I could see by the way Mike and Beth nodded at eah other that they understood the point of the exercise.

"If you don't mind doing this, it will make the data that much more meaningful."

I sensed their sincerity when they expressed their eagerness to help in any way possible. They promised to go back and look at the information again as it related to the control, Wolf's cousin.

I could hardly wait to see the official results of Gary's analysis. Mike and Beth had confirmed verbally much of what Wolf brought through in his initial visit, but a conversation wasn't scientific. Gary and his colleagues at the University of Arizona had used his valid scoring system for more than a decade of laboratory research of mediumship. I thanked them for their efforts, and they thanked me for the reading. I assured them that it was as much a gift for me as it was for them.

Within days I received an email from Dr. Gary Schwartz with an attachment. His cover email thanked me for the opportunity to review the evidence of Wolf's visit. I smiled because it was I who owed the good professor many thanks. He was one busy man. In addition to his research, he filled his days teaching classes at the university, writing books, and giving lectures around the country. What I appreciated about Gary is that we shared the same devotion, respect, and passion for what both of us referred to as "the Work."

"As you will see from the attached analysis," Gary wrote, "This visit is one of the best of its kind I have ever seen."

My heart fluttered with excitement. The kind of visit to which he referred, I knew, was an unexpected one from a spirit unbeknown to the medium beforehand. The fact that I received no feedback while receiving the information added immeasurably to the validity of the experience. Gary had been testing and researching mediums three times longer than I had been practising as one. For him to label the visit *"one of the best of its kind,"* I suddenly understood why Wolf wanted to have the information officially documented.

I clicked on the attachment. Clearly, Mike and Beth had done their work, for the caption above the large colored bar chart at the top of the Word document read, "Percent Hits and Misses for Wolf (blue) and Cousin (red)." As my eyes scanned the two bars representing hits and the two representing misses, I felt an rush of pleasure. The visual manner in which Gary presented the data made the results of his analysis immediately obvious.

In the "hit" section, Wolf's blue bar towered over the red bar like a sky scraper next to a one-story building. The numbers beneath them indicated that 73.9 percent of the evidence brought through in the unexpected visit "fit" Wolf. A mere 5.6 percent of the items fit the cousin.

The results on the "misses" side of the chart showed a near mirror image. The blue bar now sat dwarfed next to the tall red one. The data showed that only 13.0 percent of the items I sent to Mike and Beth did not fit Wolf, while 80.5 percent did not fit the cousin. The fact that the percentiles did not add up to 100 reflected the absence of scores for those items that were not rate-able. These included statements such as, "He was an old, old soul," that were impossible to validate from our Earthly perspective. [2]

On my second round of studying the results, my eyes fell on the "hits" section, but this time I frowned. The column in blue may have represented a remarkable number of clear hits, but now all I could think was, *"I was an "A" student. Seventy-four percent is only a 'C'."*

My mind traveled across the ocean to England, where I had studied mediumship with some of the best evidential mediums in the world. There,

---

[2] A summary of the data is provided in Appendix

in the hallowed halls of The Arthur Findlay College of Psychic Sciences, one wise, seasoned instructor stated, "You should not be a medium if you're a perfectionist."

I moved my cursor to the top of the screen and closed the file with a click on the big red "X." I shook my head and then smiled, forced to laugh at myself again. I had chosen to be a medium, and if I was anything, I was a perfectionist. It might not be the best combination, but I was determined to do the best I could for those in the spirit world.

A friendly inner voice reminded me of the manner in which I had received Wolf's information. It wasn't as if he had stood in the front of a classroom and shared information the way my former teachers had. Instead, his soul had come to me in the early morning darkness and whispered to me using only our blended consciousness to communicate. Considering the challenges involved, I conceded that a "C" might be acceptable after all. Still, I couldn't help but wonder what mysteries lay hidden in Wolf's unsolved messages.

CHAPTER SEVEN

Symbols And Signs

Our new coach glided effortlessly up the eight percent grade of Snoqualmie Pass on our eastbound route through the Cascades. Recreational vehicle ads show new models cruising down a highway against a backdrop of shimmering lakes and snow-capped peaks. The breathtaking view we enjoyed as we left Seattle in our rear view camera rivaled any advertisement in *Motorhome* magazine.

Ty and I would cover many miles in the coming month, but all of them as tourists. I had completed a flurry of speaking engagements in western Canada and the Pacific Northwest, and now we planned to put our hiking boots and camera to good use. The road ahead would take us into Idaho, then on to Montana, and back into Canada a second time. We especially looked forward to experiencing the Canadian Rockies in Alberta's Banff National Park.

I normally worked on my laptop during Ty's turn at the wheel. This morning, however, I sat in the passenger seat with a sheaf of papers in hand. Before leaving the campground I had received an email from Mike and Beth. It contained their detailed scoring of Wolf's unexpected visit that Gary Schwartz had used to do his analysis. I had printed out the pages before setting out and I studied them now, fascinated. The rankings and rationale that Mike and Beth provided for each item gave me new insights into the information Wolf had transmitted.

Their comments provided further validation for many of the items, but I puzzled over those that fell into the category of "misses." The Radio Flyer wagon remained a mystery, as did the item described as *"Hitting a stone with a chisel. Chiseling a message."* Mike rated this as only a "possible hit," and wrote, "Wolf tried every method of drawing and sketching." After reading his rationale, I would have rated it even lower. I didn't know why Wolf brought up chiseling messages into stone, but I felt sure it didn't concern his artwork.

In response to Wolf showing me a bird hitting a window, Mike wrote, "Years ago I was standing in the living room and witnessed a bird crash into my bay windows. Wolf might have been there." He ranked this a "3" out of 6.

Again I shook my head. I agreed with almost all of their rankings, except as they related for these two messages. I had given enough readings to know that those on the other side bring up specific memories for a reason. Mike could only speculate that Wolf had been there when the bird flew into the window. In my mind, the item only deserved a "2."

The items on the list ranked with a "1"—the clear misses—lacked written comments. I supposed there was nothing to say. None of us had any idea why Wolf would have shown me *Experiments. Like science. Beakers.* We also couldn't figure out why he would transmit, *"Über-intelligent,"* a word partly in German and partly in English. Wolf wasn't German, and he hadn't been "over intelligent."

The one low-scoring item from the unexpected visit that puzzled me the most was *"Pajamas ... Jama Mama."* In my mind, this wasn't a "miss," but a "mis-interpretation." I felt strongly that Wolf was trying to transmit a word that wasn't in my conscious mind. The syllables came through clearly, but I had nothing in my mental data bank that sounded like a jama mama in pajamas.

I looked up from the papers and stared out the coach window. My mind traveled east three thousand miles to Wolf's old stomping grounds in Plymouth, Massachusetts. Nothing I saw there filled in any of the blanks.

What were you trying to tell me? I asked him silently.

Suddenly, two piercing yellow eyes appeared before mine and stared back at me. I instinctively pulled in my chin, startled by what then expanded into a Wolf's face covering my full field of vision. The image lingered for a moment and then faded away, remaining just long enough to revive a forgotten memory.

Six months earlier I had been lying on a treatment table in the home of my friend Lynn Walker, a gifted energy worker. Lynn had helped me to enter an unusually deep state of relaxation, when a large and imposing Wolf's face appeared in my mind's eye.

"The Wolf must be your totem," Lynn told me after I dreamily described what I was seeing.

At the time, I didn't think much about it. Totems didn't figure much in my work as a medium. Ty and I had recently seen some beautiful totem poles at a park in Vancouver, but I knew little about their history or significance. Intrigued by this second unexpected vision of a wolf's face, I reached down to the floor by my seat and picked up my iPad.

A quick search of the Internet revealed that "totem" was merely another word for a "sacred symbol." I adjusted my search and found no shortage of listings for "animals as sacred symbols." Nearly every site I opened included the wolf as a totem, and each of those sites described similar characteristics for this proud animal.

One account struck me as particularly relevant. It helped me to understand why Wolf had chosen his nickname: "Wolves are highly misunderstood animals," the article stated. "In reality, wolves are friendly and social creatures. Aggression is something they avoid. Even though living in close-knit packs provides wolves with a strong sense of family, they are still able to maintain their individuality. Wolves represent the spirit of freedom."[3]

I opened the "notes" app on my iPad and typed the word "freedom." It was the one characteristic of the wolf that showed up more than any other on the various totem sites. Leaning back in my seat, I pondered the concept of symbolism. Those in the spirit world often used symbols in my readings. They could convey meaningful concepts using simple, recognizable images. The method proved to be both efficient and accurate.

An image of a labyrinth popped into my mind. According to Mike and Beth, Wolf's mention of the labyrinth was one of the major hits during their reading. I recalled that it was the yin-yang symbol at the center of the labyrinth that caught their attention. The fact that they encountered the labyrinth at the conference where we met made that piece of evidence especially significant.

Mike and Beth told me that Wolf included the yin-yang symbol in many of his drawings. He had placed it strategically at the center of the eye on his final prophetic poem. A few keystrokes on my iPad brought up a list of results for "significance of yin-yang symbol."

I was already familiar with the ancient Chinese design. My workshops included lessons about the concept of oneness and our connection with all that is. I knew that the yin-yang symbol represented the ongoing dance of

---

[3] http://www.animaltotem.com/store.html?wc=79

opposites in our current reality, united within the oneness of the circle. As I read the more detailed description of the symbol on the Internet, the words "balance" and "harmony" appeared on each site I opened.

I closed the web browser and returned to the notes app. There I added "balance and harmony" beneath the word "freedom." I studied the short list and pursed my lips. I could understand that Wolf might have been a free spirit. That seemed like a good fit, but why did he feature the yin-yang symbol in his drawings? I wondered if perhaps his life seemed out of balance and the yin-yang symbol represented an ideal.

The moment the thought of imbalance occurred to me, a wave of dizziness passed through my head. I gripped the armrest on my seat until the sensation passed. In its wake, the wolf's face flashed again before my eyes and I instantly relaxed.

You're here, aren't you?

The answer came in the form of several skipped heartbeats followed by a warm current that spread across my chest. I turned towards the driver's seat and announced softly, "Ty, Wolf is here. Do me a favor, and please don't talk for a few minutes."

Ty nodded his head without saying a word, and I felt a rush of gratitude. We had been together for years before I discovered I could communicate with the spirit world. He had married a naval officer, not a medium. Ty was even more left-brained than I used to be. I knew that many of the things I shared with him gave him pause, yet he supported me in every way.

I faced forward again, closed my eyes, and shifted my consciousness. Mike and Beth had sent me pictures of Wolf after their reading. I didn't need the photos to recognize Wolf's powerful energy. His soul was now formless. He was pure consciousness. And he was back.

Didn't I tell you I'd be around? He flashed the wolf's face before my eyes again, taking me instantly back to my session with Lynn Walker.

Have you been helping me since then? I asked. *Are you here to help me now?*

His response took me by surprise.

Cast a rune.

I felt a shiver of excitement. This had to be Wolf, and not my imagination. I never would have thought of runes to receive an answer. I had dabbled with divination tools in the past, but mostly out of curiosity. I owned a pendulum

49

and a set of Tarot cards, and I even had a Tarot app on my iPad. I enjoyed picking a card now and then for the fun of seeing if anything meaningful surfaced, but I didn't rely on the cards for advice. I had my own team of advisors on the other side, and I trusted their guidance implicitly.

I was aware that Tarot was based on the "Fool's Journey," which was a metaphor for each person's journey through life. The cards stood either for stages in that journey or for virtues and vices faced along the way. They used archetypes, character traits, and objects such as swords and wands to tell a story.

I knew little about the symbolism used in runes, however. In their reading, Beth had linked runes with the hieroglyphics Wolf had mentioned in his first visit. She said that he featured the runic alphabet in many of his drawings. I had always associated hieroglyphics with Egyptian writing, but after the conversation with Beth, I looked up the word and I learned that hieroglyphics apply to any writing system that uses symbols or pictures to denote objects or concepts. Runes do just that, so it was a valid comparison. Still, I had no idea if the runes' symbols stood for people, animals, shapes, objects, or something more arcane.

In addition to my lack of experience with runes, I faced one other challenge in carrying out Wolf's request: I didn't have any stones to cast. I glanced out the coach windows at the pine forests and mountains on both sides of the highway. The odds of finding a nearby store with a bag of runes on the shelves were not exactly encouraging.

Frustrated, I lowered my head, and my gaze fell on my iPad. Instantly my mood improved. If there was a Tarot app for tablets, surely some enterprising techie had created a rune app as well.

I clicked on the app store icon, typed "Runes" in the search box, and hit "enter." Within seconds I had my choice of seven possible programs. Aware that Wolf was patiently standing by, I quickly reviewed the features of each app. Only one claimed that it was designed specifically for the iPad and provided an experience much like that of casting actual stones. I clicked on the purchase button, entered my password, and watched as the software downloaded. The process took less than a minute. I shook my head in amazement, grateful for modern technology.

I opened the rune app and studied the home screen. A drawing of a tall tree much like the one on Burial Hill in Plymouth dominated the page. The tree sat atop an orange hill; beneath it the tree's roots spread outward. In the center of the roots a round, silver spiral swirled like a child's top spinning in slow motion. A series of sticklike letters filled a horizontal black bar spanning the top edge of the screen. Those letters looked very much like the ones I had seen in the photographs of Wolf's apartment.

I pushed an information button in the lower left corner of the screen. As I had hoped, the program seemed highly intuitive, but its creators did include a brief lesson on the art of rune casting.

"The runes are not an occult device," the description said. "Their value lies in their subtle ability to use mystical symbols and patterns common to all people to tease out wisdom buried in our subconscious minds. Focus your mind on the specific situation for which you seek guidance."[4]

I had my choice of casting one, three, or seven runes. Wolf had made it clear that I was to cast only one. The instructions directed me to contemplate the swirling well of runes while I concentrated on my situation. I counted the hieroglyphics across the top of the screen. There were twenty-four in all. Out of twenty-four stones, would the one I cast speak to me? Just as in my readings, I wouldn't stretch whatever came up just to make it fit. The symbol needed to be both timely and meaningful.

"Okay, Wolf," I said to him mentally as I stared at the gray spiral, *"You already know my questions: Have you been helping me with my work, and are you here to help me now?"*

I reached out and touched my index finger to the center of the well. The gray spiral turned into a solid orange circle. At the same time, a single stone appeared in the middle of the tree's trunk. The symbol on the stone depicted an upward-pointing arrow.

I stared at the arrow, but no insights came to me. Frustrated, I again consulted the instructions, which informed me that if I touched the stone, a window would appear with the rune's name and a detailed definition.

Even though Wolf remained silent during this process, I felt a growing sense of excitement. I knew that those on the other side could manipulate electronic devices to get our attention. My first experience with this phenomenon occurred the week after our beloved Susan's funeral when the television in our hotel room went on by itself. Many

---

[4] Runes for iPad, Netistry Corporation, Copyright 2013.

of my clients had experienced their house lights flickering or a doorbell ringing by itself shortly after a loved one passed. Wolf was one powerful soul. If he wanted to make a point with me, he could very well manipulate a set of electronic runes.

"Okay, Wolf," I thought as I touched the screen, *"Are you with me or not?"*

As promised, a window popped up. A title bar across the top read "Tiwaz." Beneath the title bar was the arrow stone with a verbal description.

"Tiwaz is the warrior rune," it began.

I bobbled my head from side to side. *Okay. I was a warrior for twenty years and I have the Combat Action Ribbon to prove it.* Was that meaningful or was it a stretch?

Possibly a stretch, I conceded, and I read on.

"It is named for the mythological warrior, Tiw, who sacrificed his hand ..."

I paused, shaking my head. This was definitely not meaningful, and it seemed a bit macabre. I wondered if I was just being silly, buying and playing with a set of runes based on a vision. Was it merely wishful thinking that Wolf was helping me with my work?

I felt a subtle nudge to read on, and so I did. My gaze moved to the end of the sentence and I gasped aloud.

Tiw had great purpose, after all, when he sacrificed his hand.

He did it *"to ensnare the giant wolf."*

My skin prickled with goose bumps as I experienced surprise mixed with awe and joy. I treasured such moments when the Universe speaks without using words. Those in spirit form don't need to say a thing. The unmistakable signs we call "synchronicity" are indications of a higher hand at work. When we're open to noticing the signs they leave us, we discover just how connected the two worlds are.

I became aware of that connection after Susan passed, and I got in the habit of asking for signs. My unseen helpers must have known I needed frequent confirmation. Meaningful synchronicities occurred with enough frequency that Ty no longer reacted to or questioned my astonished outbursts. He had learned that if he simply waited, I would fill him in after I gathered my wits.

I turned to him now and explained that I had asked Wolf if he was helping me with my work.

"He told me to cast a rune," I said, "so I downloaded a rune app onto my iPad."

Ty gave a small chuckle. "That was handy."

"I had no idea what kind of symbolism runes used," I continued. "For all I knew, they could have referred to shapes, or people, or just about anything. But listen to the one that turned up ..."

I read the description of the Tiwaz rune. When I reached the part about the wolf, Ty jerked his head in my direction, taking his gaze off the road just long enough for me to see the surprise in his eyes.

I grinned back. "Pretty cool, huh?"

"Yeah," he nodded thoughtfully.

I could tell by the set of his mouth that he was trying to digest this latest "coincidence."

"There are twenty four stones in a set of runes," I explained, adding, "The number twenty-four came up in his reading, and what are the chances of the one I cast having a reference to a wolf?"

"Like you said, it's pretty cool."

I realized I hadn't read the rest of the card's description to find out what the warrior rune represented. I refreshed the screen and discovered that Tiwaz embodied the virtues of courage, integrity, and duty. I couldn't help but smile. The three core values of every Navy man and woman are honor, courage, and commitment.

According to the write-up, the appearance of Tiwaz indicated the need for courage, as victory is assured if one's heart remains true. It further reminded the one who cast the rune that every great movement begins with one person who is willing to take a risk in order to do what's right.

Those who knew about my former military career often remarked about the courage it must take for me to work now as a medium. I tended to dismiss their praise. I was simply doing what I believed was my very special duty. For twenty years I served my country. My current work was simply another way of serving, albeit at a higher level. Whether or not I agreed with the rune's description of being courageous, I certainly was trying to do the right thing.

I looked up from my iPad and noticed that the scenery had gradually changed during the past hour since the wolf's face appeared and I had become absorbed in rune symbolism. The green forests and steep slopes of the Cascades had slipped away behind us as we entered the more arid

Columbia plateau. I glanced at my watch. It was my turn to take the wheel.

I closed the cover on my iPad and told Ty I was ready to drive. He asked if I was sure I could concentrate. I thought of Wolf, who I knew was now watching over my shoulder, and assured him that I was fine.

CHAPTER EIGHT

Pieces Of The Puzzle

My mother's feet and legs came into view first. I ducked down to see the rest of her as the escalator carried me to the baggage claim level. She saw me the moment my eyes locked on hers and she broke into a broad smile that mirrored my own. I picked up my pace and moments later enjoyed our first hug in three months.

There were times in my Navy career when my overseas assignments kept us apart for almost a year. Although my mother and I now lived only three miles apart in Florida, Ty and I left her to travel five months out of the year. These separations seemed much longer now that Mom was in her eighties and living alone, so I planned a one-week visit home half-way through each summer's tour. Normally the timing worked out just right for us to celebrate our mutual August birthday in person. This year, however, our travel schedule required us to be in a remote area on my birthday. To save on flight costs, I traveled home a week early while Ty stayed with the puppies near the airport in Spokane, Washington.

After hugging my mother at the airport, I turned and gave a heart-felt hug to our dear friends Lynn and Bailey Spence. Even though Mom insisted she could drive the seventy miles to the Orlando airport by herself, I thanked Lynn and Bailey for accompanying her. My baggage arrived quickly, and within minutes we were headed north on the Florida turnpike in our chauffeur's perky Prius.

It didn't take long to catch up on each other's latest news. Mom and I spoke daily by phone, and Lynn and I often emailed each other. The car soon grew quiet, and I checked my watch. Since we still had a good forty-five minutes left to go, I said, "I'd love to share with you some really cool things that have been happening with a young man named Wolf who is on the other side."

Bailey glanced in the rear view mirror and Lynn turned sideways in the passenger seat. Her eagerness was very much in evidence and it matched my mother's, who was sitting on my right. Lynn and Bailey shared my keen interest in the afterlife, and they always wanted to hear the latest updates about my work. My mother also loved my stories, even if she didn't always understand the metaphysical concepts.

I started at the beginning and described meeting Mike Pasakarnis at the A.R.E. conference. I then told them about Wolf's poem and the drawing of the two red roses that his parents had left at the base of the tree. They reacted with the same astonishment as Ty and I did the first time we heard this remarkable tale.

Mike and Beth had given me permission to speak freely with others about their son, so I continued with the details of Wolf's unexpected visit. The miles clicked off as I filled them in on the evidence from the Skype reading.

We discussed the feedback from Gary Schwartz, and they laughed at my dissatisfaction with the 74 percent score. I explained that my frustration arose from the fact that most of the items that received a low score were not necessarily wrong. They simply held no obvious meaning for Wolf's parents. I used the Radio Flyer wagon as an example of one of the more mystifying details.

We arrived home just as I finished describing Wolf's recent appearance in the coach. I could tell that everyone wanted to hear more, and I promised I would keep them current if and when Wolf paid me another visit.

I said goodnight and made arrangements to get together with my mother the next day. It felt strange to walk into my house and not be greeted by Ty and two tail-wagging dachshunds. It felt even stranger to crawl into our big bed alone. I called to let Ty know I had arrived safe and sound, and soon fell fast asleep.

The next morning I woke up later than usual due to the three-hour change in time zones. I began my day with my morning meditation, and then turned on my computer to check for email. I was surprised to see four new messages from Lynn Spence after saying goodbye to her less than twelve hours earlier. The first message showed a transmission time of 7:51.

"Hope you slept well," Lynn wrote. "Can't get Wolf off my mind."

I smiled, both amused and touched that Lynn would still be thinking about him.

"There was a movie named *Radio Flyer* that came out several years ago," she wrote further. "I watched the trailer this morning, but it wasn't much help. It's about two brothers and a 'sad period' in their lives. I haven't seen the whole movie. I don't know if there's anything in there that might help. I'll look some more later. I have aerobics this morning."

I was surprised but pleased that Lynn had taken the time to look into one of the mysteries from Wolf's visit. I wondered what happened to her aerobics class when I saw that her next email was sent a little more than an hour later.

"In the movie," she said, referring to the *Radio Flyer* film, "the mother is Mary and step-father is Jack. Still looking..."

Three minutes later she wrote, "Okay, maybe I'm over the edge here, but please read this review by Roger Ebert." She provided a link and commented, "He hates the movie, but some of the things he said hit home. Nothing you said last night mentioned problems at home, but the movie starts with a divorce and goes from there."

I went from amusement to curiosity, with a sense that Lynn might not be over the edge at all. I knew that Wolf's parents had divorced, and I could check to see if his biological mother had remarried.

Lynn's third email continued, "At some point, Ebert says, 'Heroes have to take chances.' In my mind, Wolf's coming here was a big chance, and he took that chance and suffered all the abuse our misguided Earthlings heaped on him simply because he was different. In the movie, the little boy rigs his wagon so he can fly away. Maybe Wolf arranged the lightning as his escape. Freedom. Bingo?"

I pursed my lips and reread the words. They seemed surprisingly plausible. I found it especially curious that she used the word "bingo." The same word came up in Wolf's reading, but I hadn't shared that with her.

Her final email, sent only three minutes after the previous message, contained one simple line: "One reviewer calls the movie 'schizoid.'"

I did a small double-take. The unusual choice of words was most likely a coincidence, but Lynn had piqued my curiosity enough to follow the link she provided. The similarities in the details between Wolf's life and the movie about a Radio Flyer wagon were hard to ignore. When I read further and learned that the movie's main character was named Mike, just like Wolf, I knew I had to call Mike and Beth.

I didn't have to look up their phone number. I had spoken with them only a few days earlier after the incident in the coach with Wolf and the runes. I usually don't keep in touch with clients, but in Wolf's case, he seemed to be doing everything in his power to connect us. I pulled up the list of recent phone calls in my iPhone and clicked on the one with a Massachusetts area code. I chuckled when Mike greeted me by name.

"How're you doing, Suzanne?"

"Hi, Mike," I said, "Caller ID is a wonderful thing, isn't it?"

"Yeah," he replied, "What's up? Did Wolf visit you again?"

"Not exactly, but I think a friend of mine might have solved the Radio Flyer mystery. Is Beth there, too?"

"I'm here," Beth said, already on the line.

I greeted her and smiled. She and Mike obviously loved Wolf as much as they clearly loved each other.

I told them about sharing Wolf's story with Lynn and Bailey and described how Lynn had taken it upon herself to do some detective work.

"I know that you're divorced from Wolf's biological mother," I said to Mike. "But did she remarry?"

"Yes, she did," he replied.

"All right, and pardon me for getting personal, but do you know if there was any conflict between Wolf and his step-father?"

"He did mention that, yes." Mike said.

I slowly exhaled a breath. "Wow. Well, listen to this: There was a movie a while back called 'Radio Flyer.' It's about a young boy named 'Mike.' I paused to let them absorb that.

"His parents get a divorce," I continued. "His mother remarries, and there's some conflict with the step-father. The main theme of the movie is how this little boy, Mike, wants to put wings on his red wagon so it will fly. All he wants to do is use that Radio Flyer wagon to *go home to where he's loved.*"

I paused and waited. After long moments of silence, Mike and Beth said in perfect unison, "Wow."

"Yeah, 'wow,'" I echoed. "That was one of the things Wolf stressed in his reading: *'It was like going home to draw these things; like going home.'* The red wagon fits right in with the theme of the hot air balloon he showed me and the parachute with the straps that kept him chained to this earthly home."

I didn't mention the reviewer who called the movie "schizoid." There were enough other things that fit perfectly with Wolf's life to convince us that Lynn had solved the riddle of the red wagon. I emailed my friend as soon as I got off the phone.

"All of the details fit," I wrote. "You said it: bingo. Thank you for being the detective. I hope this blows you away as much as it does me."

She must have been sitting at her computer, because she immediately wrote back. She admitted to having being awake most of the night puzzling over the mystery of the red wagon. "I never say 'bingo,'" she wrote. "When I put that in the email I deleted the bingo, but then, for some reason, I put it back."

To me, her use of the word confirmed my belief that our thoughts are often put there by helpers on the other side. I felt sure that Wolf had guided Lynn to write "bingo" so that I would know he was working with her. I wrote back one final time and thanked her for her persistence. We both agreed that Spirit had picked the right person to solve this piece of the puzzle.

It was too early to call Ty on the West Coast. I sent him a quick email to wish him a good morning, and then called my mother to tell her I would stop by after visiting my friend, Gail. I showered, dressed, and drove the familiar route to Gail's neighborhood. The two-mile drive took me past a large Barnes and Noble bookstore.

The proximity of the store was one of the major selling points in choosing our home. Ty and I are both book junkies. Before I became aware of my connection with the other side, we would often stop at the book store to browse and check out new releases. The more I tuned in to higher guidance, however, the more I discovered that if there were a book I was supposed to read, I would be led to it by Spirit. I could drive past the store a dozen times and feel no desire to shop; but if there were a book on the shelves earmarked for me, I felt a magnetic pull to go inside and find it.

This particular morning, the unseen magnet pulled with an intensity that surprised me. I drove past without stopping, and continued on to Gail's house. I only had five days to catch up with old friends, so I decided to multi-task. Gail had a book collection that rivaled my own, so I invited her to go with me to Barnes and Noble. She readily agreed.

We walked into the store and I headed on auto-pilot for the metaphysics section in the back. I was grateful to see a healthy re-order of my memoir,

Messages of Hope, on the shelves. Normally I would take the newly arrived copies to the service counter and ask the manager if she wanted me to inscribe them. Today I deferred, filled with the sense that there was another book there that had my name on it.

Finding that book would be a two-step process. I simply needed to stand back and scan the titles of the books lining the shelves and piled on the tables. Much like running my hand over a smooth surface until my fingers felt a bump, I would move my eyes from book to book until I felt a "catch." Then I would scan the book's contents and wait for a feeling that told me, "*This is the one.*"

The metaphysics section covered a thirty-foot wall of shelves that divided the music department from the rest of the store. I moved past the unit that held *Messages of Hope* and began my scan of the titles. One book caught my eye, and I pulled it from the shelf. Its contents didn't speak to me, so I returned it and stood back to scan some more. Although curious and excited to find out what book awaited me, I felt relaxed as I moved my eyes from one title to the next.

Suddenly, my body went on high alert. My brain rifled through its memory bank to find a match for what had just happened, but it came back with "*no results.*"

A book on the shelf had moved.

Shocked, I turned my head ninety degrees to the left and dropped my gaze to the floor. My thoughts whirled as I replayed the moment in my mind. In the space of less than a second, one of the books moved a half inch to the right and then immediately returned to its original position. I not only saw it move, but I heard it. It made the distinctive "*sh-sh*" sound that the pages would make if someone had physically slid the book to the right, and then back again.

I raised my eyes and turned back to face forward. I was not exactly sure which book had moved, but I need not have wondered. The moment my eyes fell on the shelf in question, the book moved again. In a perfect re-enactment, the book jogged one half inch to the right and then back to the left. I clearly heard the accompanying swish of the pages as they brushed the shelf.

I glanced around me to see if anyone else had witnessed this highly unusual phenomenon. As it was early in the day, the store was nearly empty.

I took in a deep breath and released it slowly. As I returned my gaze to the shelf, a new understanding settled over me. Even if someone had been standing directly beside me, they would not have seen what I just saw. At an intuitive level, I knew that what I had witnessed was an illusion, but I also knew that it was a very deliberate illusion, inspired by someone trying to get my attention.

Based on my understanding of science and spirit communication, it made perfect sense. Everything is energy. Everything that exists, be it physical objects, physical sensations, thoughts, or emotions, carries a unique frequency. The brain is nothing more than a frequency analyzer. It receives electrical signals from the five senses and translates them into concepts the human mind can understand.

Those in the spirit world communicate with me by exchanging waves of information-carrying energy. They send me thought waves and visual images, but they also use my body to show me how a loved one passed. By simply manipulating frequencies, they replicate highly specific signals that my brain interprets as an actual symptom.

I thought of the many ways that my body gives me evidence in a reading. My heart palpitates if the spirit with whom I communicate had heart problems while in human form. I experience actual stabbing pains, back aches, dizziness, tingling, shortness of breath, and other physical sensations that match what a person suffered while here on Earth. All of the signs come on suddenly, and disappear the moment I pass the information on to a client. While these events are at times disconcerting and uncomfortable, I welcome them for the irrefutable evidence they provide of the presence of spirit.

I stared at the book and willed it to move again, but the magical moment had passed. I recalled that magicians were often called "masters of illusion," and I realized that those on the other side were masters of manipulating consciousness. To make the book appear to move, they only needed to manipulate my field of vision. To produce the auditory experience, they created a frequency that my brain recognized as a swishing sound.

The result was an illusion, and I couldn't help but see the irony. Many of the books on the shelves before me claimed that our physical reality is an illusion. While we humans balk at such claims, I realized that in a way they were true. Our world appears "real" and solid, but it's really just a hive of vibrating energy. Illusion or not, perception is reality, and this world is very real to those of us living in it.

As I processed this expansion of my personal reality, my initial shock turned to delight. I regularly prayed to "see with new eyes," and I had just experienced a sight that was both new and unique. I leaned in now to read the writing along the spine of the book. I recognized the name Erich von Däniken as the author of the mega best-seller, *Chariot of the Gods*, but I had never seen this—his latest title—*Twilight of the Gods*.

I reached out and pulled the book from the shelf. When I turned it face up in my hands and read the subtitle, my delight instantly turned to disappointment. *Twilight of the Gods* dealt with the Mayan calendar "and the Return of the Extraterrestrials."

Dejectedly, I shook my head. The Mayan calendar was old news. The circular stone that covered a period of time referred to as the Great Cycle came to an end on December 21ˢᵗ, 2012. The Mayans believed that the universe is destroyed at the end of each universal cycle. A large number of doomsday theorists warned that our world would end on that fateful date. Happily, 2012 came and went, and Earth had survived.

As for extraterrestrials, I tried to stay away from anything to do with aliens. I wondered why the spirit world would go to such effort to bring my attention to such a controversial topic. Then I remembered Wolf's reading. *"This is where I come from,"* he said, when showing me images of triangles, spirals, and circles that reminded me of planets.

At the time, I admitted to Mike and Beth that what I was sensing from Wolf stretched my belief system. I had no personal experience with extraterrestrials. My beliefs had not changed, but if I had learned anything from working with higher consciousness, it was the value in remaining open-minded.

I turned the cover and began to browse through the fore pages. Most of the books I read had to do with spirituality, science, or consciousness studies. I saw nothing related to any of these topics in either the table of contents or the foreword. I paged ahead to the preface hoping to find some connection with Wolf or his reading.

I scanned the first page in speed-reading style, taking in only a few words at a time. My eyes were moving rapidly down the first paragraph when suddenly they stopped, drawn like a magnet to one special name: "Archangel Michael." My heart flip-flopped, just as it had at the start of Wolf's reading with Mike and Beth.

I flashed back to a day earlier in the year when I had received a special visit from Archangel Michael. At the time, I felt disbelief. Archangels simply didn't fit into my belief system, but the powerful presence was undeniable. I knew enough to be open-minded, so I picked up my notebook and pen. He proceeded to share insights about my work, which I wrote down exactly as I heard them. Before fading away, he shared a series of unusual words and phrases that at the time made no sense to me.

Worried that my husband might think I had gone completely over the edge, I didn't tell him about that early morning visit. Later the same day, Ty and I crossed paths with two strangers who matched precisely the phrases and descriptions given to me in meditation.

Based on the stunning evidence from that memorable morning, I could no longer deny that archangels exist. Not only did I tell Ty about the visit, but I incorporated the story into my public presentations. I had a date-stamped copy of the notes made that morning in meditation and photos of the couple we met. Not a single skeptic attempted to discount the encounter. The evidence was, in a word, irrefutable.

As I stared at Archangel Michael's name in the preface, I remembered the initial disbelief I felt when he revealed his identity. It was the same disappointment I'd felt moments earlier when I read the subtitle of von Däniken's book. In the case of Archangel Michael, my open-mindedness led to a change in my belief system and a major expansion of consciousness. I sensed that once again I was being nudged by another Michael who went by the nickname "Wolf" to remain open and receptive to new experiences. After all, the book had moved. Twice.

My gaze fell on the last sentence of the page. I smiled at the words, knowing then with certainty that I was meant to buy this book. "Everything is possible," von Däniken wrote, "—even the impossible."

I left the store with Gail, but I didn't mention what had happened in the metaphysical section. She knew about my connection with Spirit, but I needed time to process the event. As much as I wanted to go straight home and find out what the book had to teach me, I put it aside until later. I only had a few days at home before leaving for another two months. I wanted to fill every minute with my mother and friends.

At the end of a full day, I crawled into bed and let out a sigh. Time was passing far too quickly. As tired as I was, I wanted to read at least a few paragraphs of my new book. I felt a sense of excited anticipation as I picked up *Twilight of the Gods* and turned to the first page. I read no more than two sentences when I clearly heard a voice whisper, *Go straight to the pictures.*

I felt no presence. I simply heard the voice. But this kind of strong guidance came often to me, and I had learned to trust it. I closed the book and glanced at the edge of the pages. Sure enough, a dark, narrow strip down the middle indicated a center section of photographs. I fanned through the book until I came to the first picture.

The full-page, color photo showed a large stone monolith standing atop a cement slab set on rich, red soil. Purple hued mountains in the distance formed a backdrop for the stone figure that appeared to be at least ten feet tall. A series of circles and spirals covered the statue's arms, waist, and legs.

Four words in large font and white script at the top of the page stood out from the smaller font of the photo's caption. "Images from Puma Punku," read the title. I recognized the name of an archeological site in Bolivia that some friends had visited the year before. They shared their scrapbook with us after their trip, but I was sure I had never seen the statue shown on the page. Curious, I moved my eyes down a line and read the photo's caption.

I'm sure that even my ever-cool husband would have been startled by my sudden intake of breath. I stared at the page, incredulous. According to the caption, the photo depicted the Andean fertility goddess, *Pachamama.* She was covered with messages chiseled in stone.

My heart swelled at the thought of Wolf trying so very hard to get me to hear him correctly. *"Pachamama,"* he said repeatedly the morning he first appeared, but the name meant nothing to me at the time. Instead, my brain connected the incoming signal with the only sounds that made any sense, and I wrote, *"Pajamas. Jama Mama."*

I could feel Wolf rejoicing.

Yes, I got it. I finally got it. *Thank you!*

I glanced at the clock on the night stand. It was too late to call Mike and Beth. The book had moved for a reason. It was Wolf who led me to it, and he didn't want me wasting my time going through pages of text. He sent me straight to one very meaningful photo.

I had only intended to read a few pages and then turn out the light, but now my mind raced. I was too keyed up to sleep even if I had wanted to. Thanks to my friend Lynn playing detective, we solved the Radio Flyer mystery. Now two more pieces of Wolf's puzzle had fallen neatly into place: Pachamama and the messages chiseled in stone. I didn't yet know what the messages meant, but I had a feeling that one very determined soul was going to make sure I found out.

CHAPTER NINE

Evidence

I continued to read *Twilight of the Gods* until well after midnight. After reading a few pages, I would refer to the photographs bound into the middle of the book. Many of the images reminded me of Wolf's drawings that Mike had sent me by email earlier in the week. Round faces with alien eyes drawn by Wolf's hand stared back at me from stone heads mounted on the walls of Puma Punku more than a thousand years before Wolf walked on this Earth.

When I turned to page 28, I found a black and white photo of The Gateway to the Sun, a monolithic portal discovered at the archeological site of Tiwanaku, high up in the Bolivian Andes. The photo brought an image to mind that gave me a physical jolt. I jumped out of bed, crossed the bedroom, and picked up a stack of Hemi-Sync CDs from the corner of my dresser. I sifted through them until I found the one I was seeking.

I had bought the collection of music at a retreat the previous January and had copied it to my iPhone. For an unknown reason, three days earlier I was drawn to play the one I now held in my hand. Each time I heard the mystical melodies, my heart seemed to expand. I couldn't get enough of the blissful feelings they engendered. During my visit home I had played the CD over and over again, forsaking all other music in the process. However, I didn't make the connection that the music that so mesmerized me was Andean until I saw the picture in the book profiling the Mayan calendar.

I looked down at the case cover and shook my head in amazement. The title of the CD was *Portal to Eternity*. Against a backdrop of cerulean sky stood a large stone archway of the same proportions as the Gateway to the Sun in von Däniken's book. White stars and circular orbs danced under the arches, giving the scene an otherworldly feel. The caption beneath the portal read, "Dissolve the barrier between here and there."

66

I climbed back into bed hearing echoes of Wolf's words. *"This is where I come from. It was like going home to draw these things."*

I picked up my pen and wrote "Portal to Eternity" across the photograph of the Gateway to the Sun. Like the statue of Pachamama, the Gateway to the Sun was covered with messages *chiseled in stone*, a phrase I clearly heard from Wolf in his unexpected visit.

On the facing page I learned that according to archaeologist Dr. Edmund Kiss, the engravings on the sun gate represented some kind of calendar. Dr. Kiss claimed that the ancient people who invented the calendar "belonged to a higher civilization than ours." The last sentence on the page stated that the calendar provides us with "incontrovertible scientific evidence."

From my first days of working as a medium, I referred to the nuggets of information I received from those on the other side as "evidence." To confirm that the evidence was incontrovertible, I worked closely with a highly respected scientist. Now I couldn't shake the feeling that when Wolf spoke of Pachamama and messages chiseled in stone, he knew they wouldn't make sense at first. He knew that I would be led to this book and to these magical moments of discovery.

When I could no longer keep my eyes open, I turned out the light. I don't know how long I had been asleep when Wolf's presence awoke me. *"It is all about cosmic evolution,"* he said. *"Love."*

Feeling lightheaded, I rolled onto my side, scribbled the words onto my notepad, and thanked him for his visit. As my digital bedside clock registered three o'clock, I listened carefully to the silence. I distinctly heard the name *"Enoch"* and I wrote it down. That one word was soon followed by a lengthier message which I also dutifully recorded.

I waited for more words, but heard nothing. His presence faded away, and I drifted back to sleep.

In the morning, as soon as I finished my daily meditation, I continued reading *Twilight of the Gods*. I turned a few pages and stopped short. The name "Enoch" stared back at me from the page, jogging a hazy memory. I remembered some kind of communication in the dark of night, and went to retrieve my notepad from the bedroom. When I saw the words I'd written, I smiled, remembering more clearly Wolf's brief visit.

Any notion that hearing and reading the name "Enoch" might be a coincidence disappeared when von Däniken referenced the name several more times in the ensuing pages. I tried to remember the last time I had heard or encountered anything with the name Enoch in it. The answer, if there was one, was buried too far back in my memory to recall. I realized that just like his mention of Pachamama, Wolf had known I would find Enoch in the book. This was no coincidence; rather it was evidence to validate the fact that he had, indeed, visited me in the middle of the night.

My gaze fell on the longer message that he transmitted just after I heard the name "Enoch." The words held far more meaning for me now, and my heart swelled with gratitude.

"All of these synchronicities are not just to prove my existence," Wolf had said, *"but to continue the work."*

Von Däniken certainly had a passion for his work, I learned. His in-depth research into ancient sites that could not have been constructed by its Stone Age inhabitants made the thought of extra-terrestrials more palatable than when I first picked up his book. I read, fascinated by the subject matter, but still not understanding why Wolf had led me to the book.

I glanced at the clock and gave a start. I was supposed to meet my mother for breakfast in less than half an hour, but I couldn't shake the urge to keep reading. I picked up my cell phone and dialed her number. Happily, she didn't mind postponing breakfast to lunch.

I moved to the kitchen and chuckled when I opened the refrigerator. It was bare-bones empty. The cupboards held nothing but a few dusty cans that we hadn't deemed worthy to take with us in the coach. I shuffled back to the bedroom and dug through the carry-on luggage that lay open on the floor by the bed. The banana that I had put in the bag three days earlier was now a mushy, black mess. I made a face and tossed it in the trash can.

From my carry-on I pulled out a tiny package of honey roasted nuts with a jet on the wrapper and a bag of Cheezits that looked as if it had been worked over by a rolling pin. I retrieved von Däniken's book and hauled my feast of peanuts and Cheezit crumbs to the living room couch.

In between bites of breakfast I picked up my pen to underline phrases of interest in the book. When I turned to page 45, the first paragraph caught my eye. "Anyone who visited the ruins of Tiwanaku 400 years ago would have felt overawed by the mighty constructions," von Däniken wrote. "These days you might even say overwhelmed."

As I read the words "overawed" and "overwhelmed," I was transported back to my college German class. In my mind's eye I saw my professor writing the word "over" on the blackboard, beside which he wrote the German translation, "*über*."

Unlike the foreign name Enoch, which I could not recall hearing in recent history, I remembered hearing "über" less than a week earlier when Wolf first visited. Each time I reviewed the list of evidence from that initial visit, the term "über-intelligent" stood out as a "miss."

A momentary bout of dizziness caught me off guard, and I shook my head to clear it. The vertigo passed, but my energy-field had shifted. I realized I was no longer alone in the house.

"*Look at the bibliography*," Wolf directed.

I had learned in my Navy days to obey orders without question. This one was so clear that I immediately thumbed to the back of the book. When I found the bibliography, I gaped in surprise. A few of the titles were in English, some were in Spanish or French, but most were in German. I turned page after page in the lengthy list of references and saw words I hadn't seen since college German class. There, in the book that moved, I found titles such as *Mehr Klarheit über die Schriftrollen* and *Über die Religion der vorislamischen Araber*.

I sat back and smiled, enjoying yet another magical moment with Wolf, and I felt him smiling back.

I had assumed that Erich von Däniken was an American author. A few quick clicks on the iPad at my side opened his website. The portal gave viewers a choice of language, and German had top billing. I clicked on "English" to enter the site, and navigated to the page profiling von Däniken's biography.

Sure enough, he was born in Switzerland, not in the United States. He had attended a German-speaking school in his youth, and now lived in a small Swiss village. He was fluent in four languages, was an avid researcher, and was the recipient of multiple awards, including an honorary doctorate. Erich von Däniken was obviously an intelligent man. In fact, I realized, one could say without stretching the facts that he was *über-intelligent*.

One of the helpful hints I had learned in working with Spirit was to pay attention to things that caught my attention, no matter how subtle. I now realized that Wolf had made the words "overawed" and "overwhelmed" stand out in my mind when I read them. Once he had my attention, he showed me the image of the professor at the blackboard, and then sent me directly to the bibliography.

I turned back to the page I'd been reading when I became aware of Wolf's presence and circled the two meaningful words. Visitors to Tiwanaku 400 years ago may have been overawed and overwhelmed. Working with Wolf was giving me a taste of just how overwhelmed they must have felt.

I read on, fascinated to find material that was completely new to me and that spoke to the possible origins of sacred sites around the world. In chapter two, von Däniken abruptly shifted from writing about ancient activities in the Andes to modern-day events in Great Britain. He described both the excitement and controversy of English experiments in which scientists are trying to cross-breed human genetic material with that of animals. While shocking, this kind of cross-breeding is nothing new, von Däniken wrote.

Once again several words seemed to jump off the page as if highlighted. I recalled that Wolf had transmitted something about experiments in his early morning visit. He had mentioned science and beakers, and accompanied these terms with the image of mad scientists experimenting in a garage. Mike and Beth had no idea why Wolf would have been discussing such a subject. I, in turn, had no idea why von Däniken was doing the same thing in this new chapter.

Two pages later, he got to the point. He explained that what is being done today in England was in fact being done thousands of years ago. To back up his claim, he quoted ancient witnesses such as the Greek historian Eusabius, who died in 339 AD. According to Eusabius, during those ancient times the so-called gods who visited Earth created monstrous beasts that were part man and part animal. Von Däniken admitted that the claims seemed preposterous until one studied the artifacts that have survived from these periods. He referenced the ancient reliefs on columns and sculptures in major museums around the world. These reliefs depicted hybrid creatures, or "chimeras." Archaeologists call them "winged geniuses."

A black and white photo of one such creature dominated the facing page. It stood tall like a human and was draped in a robe with a sash. The head featured a long, pointed beak and an oversized eye. Large wings sprouted from the back of the robe. The creature reached out its human arms and hands as if plucking flowers from a tree at the edge of the carving. The caption read, *"Winged geniuses working by the tree of life."*

As I studied the picture, Wolf whispered in my ear.

"Look at my drawings."

Mike had sent me several of Wolf's sketches during the past few days, but none of them resembled the photo in the book. *"Are there any of winged beings?"* I asked him silently.

I sensed him nodding in response, and I heard, *"Flying, flying."*

I reached in my pocket, pulled out my cell phone, and placed a call to Mike Pasakarnis. His phone rang four times and when it went to voicemail I briefly summarized how I had found several more of the missing pieces from Wolf's visit in a new book that he had led me to.

"Wolf is here with me right now," I said. "He's telling me that some of his drawings depict winged creatures. If you can scan them and send them to me by email as soon as possible, I'd really appreciate it." I thanked him and promised to talk to both him and Beth soon.

I hung up the phone and realized that I hadn't bothered to ask if Wolf had drawn winged creatures. I didn't need to ask. I knew with an absolute certainty that he had. It was only a matter of waiting for Mike to send them. I looked at my watch and noted that it was already time to leave for lunch. I set the book on top of my iPad and transmitted a silent *"Thank you"* to Wolf before heading out the door.

Two hours later, after enjoying a pleasant meal with my mother, I returned to the house. I walked straight to my laptop and pulled up my email. To my delight, Mike's name appeared at the top of the list of new messages. A paperclip icon indicated that he had included an attachment. I clicked on the email and read the brief note.

"Wolf had lots of drawings of winged creatures," Mike wrote. "I've attached a few here." I smiled when I read his closing comment: "Beth and I were thinking how the score keeps going up ... it's like Wolf wants to prove every word he shared. But wait, aren't you the one who asks for proof and more?"

I definitely insisted on the evidence, and Wolf seemed to know that. The drawings Mike sent left no doubt. The moment the first one opened on my screen, I felt his presence near me.

"Do you see?" he said without words. And how could I not?

Like the winged genius in *Twilight of the Gods*, Wolf's winged creature stood tall like a human, with the same proportions as the ancient carving. Its head was long, narrow, and pointed like the *winged genius's* beak. Both figures faced left, shown in profile. Both wore a long robe with a sash. Both had large wings, fringed hair, and long fingers. Even the most skeptical critic could see the remarkable similarities.

Mike was right. We might need to have Dr. Schwartz rescore the unexpected visit if Wolf was going to keep filling in the missing pieces of the puzzle. The mystery wasn't solved yet, though. As I picked up the book and studied the cover, I shook my head in confusion. Mayans, extraterrestrials, and ancient gods . . . He was trying to show us something. That much was clear, but the message remained lost in the complexities.

"What is this all about?" I asked Wolf silently.

His answer came in words this time, and I wrote them down verbatim. *"We are not gods, not deities, not to be revered. Just a higher vibration, here to teach love."*

Yes, and so am I, I thought. *So are all of us.*

The recurring theme in the messages I receive from Spirit each morning in meditation is the oneness of all creation. Working as a medium has shown me how very connected we are with All That Is. Our world is just a tiny part of a far greater world, and the two worlds are intricately interconnected. One by one Wolf was helping to reveal the connections. I wasn't sure how they would all come together, but I had no doubt that Wolf's message would bring us back to love.

CHAPTER TEN

Toward The Light

Many people who die and return to tell about it describe similar visions. A common experience is that of passing through a tunnel, drawn irresistibly onward by a bright light. Two days after returning to Ty from my trip home I experienced first-hand a small taste of what it must be like to have a near-death experience.

As darkness enveloped me, I reminded myself that it was only a temporary phenomenon. I traveled onward, trying to ignore the cold, damp chill and keep my fears at bay. The tunnel seemed endless, but suddenly I saw a glimmer of brightness. Relief flooded through my body, and I picked up my pace as the round light grew ever larger. Passing through an arched portal, I took in a breath, stunned by the contrast between the blackness behind me and the bright sunlight that instantly raised the temperature twenty degrees.

It was Ty's idea to make this most unusual bike ride. He had learned about the Hiawatha Trail while planning our route from Washington to Montana. I looked forward to experiencing what the guide book described as one of the most scenic bike rides in the country. The abandoned rail bed traversed nine tunnels and seven bridges on its way across the Montana/Idaho state line. The first and longest of the tunnels tested the mettle of even the hardiest cyclist with its 1.7 miles of unlighted, puddle-filled roadway.

The trail before us now wound downhill through a thick forest of lodgepole pines set against the majestic backdrop of the Bitterroot Mountains. Route I-90 seemed a world away as we surveyed a vast expanse of primeval wilderness. From our vantage point at the exit of the long Taft Tunnel, the only man-made structures in sight were several tall trestles crossing the St. Regis River far below from where we stood.

A sudden screech broke the pristine, almost sacred silence.

"Hand me the camera," Ty said. "It's a red-tailed hawk."

My gaze followed to where he was pointing as I lifted the camera's strap from around my neck.

Ty leaned his bike against a tree and wandered off to try to find a good angle.

As I watched the hawk circling, I admired its beauty. Its rust-colored tail fanned out in a perfect semi-circle behind its broad, brown and white wings. I marveled at the timing of the bird's visit. Hours earlier I had received an email from Beth in which the main subject was a hawk.

The latest revelations about Wolf's initial visit from The Book That Moved had prompted her to do some detective work of her own. She stumbled upon a book called *Animal Speak: The Spiritual and Magical Powers of Creatures Great and Small*, written by Ted Andrews and published by Llewellyn Publications. I thought it sounded like a fitting find for a veterinarian. The book listed the spiritual significance of more than a hundred different animals, birds, insects, and reptiles.

"I read about wolf totems," Beth wrote in her email, "but I was also drawn to look up the hawk. You mentioned that Wolf watches over us like a hawk."

I well remembered the reference. In his initial visit he made me underline the word as if it were significant. I recalled writing down "soaring" as Wolf gave me the feeling of a bird in flight just before he showed me a bird flying into a window. Unfortunately, neither the hawk nor the image of a bird hitting a window had conjured up any specific memories for Mike and Beth.

In her recent email Beth shared the long-held belief that the hawk as a totem represented visionary power and guardianship.

"More striking is what followed the description about the number 14," Beth wrote, "since that number came to you early in your first visit from Wolf."

She then quoted the book verbatim: "Hawks can live up to 14 years in the wild."

I shook my head in denial. I saw no connection between the life span of a hawk and Wolf's life. My thoughts about the number's relevance changed, however, as I read the more detailed explanation.

"This number is significant because the 14th card in the tarot deck is the card that represents the teaching of higher expressions of psychic work and vision. It holds the keys to higher levels of consciousness."

Beth had my attention now. Ever since I discovered my ability to communicate with the spirit world, one of my top goals was to improve my attunement with those on the other side. I dedicated my studies and daily meditations to achieving higher levels of consciousness.

"I think a lot of Wolf's messages have a deeper meaning than we can relate to right now within the confines of what we perceive to be our reality," Beth wrote. "Maybe more answers will be revealed as we go further down this path with his guidance."

Now as the red-tailed hawk flew away and Ty and I headed down the path on our bikes, I wondered if Wolf's early morning message would reveal anything about my own visionary powers. One thing was certain: if my psychic abilities had been better, we would not have driven our coach down the dirt and gravel road to the trailhead. We enjoyed the scenic bike trail, but at the end of the ride we faced a quarter inch of dust on the coach.

That evening we crossed from Idaho into Montana. While camping in the town of St. Regis, I received a phone call from a number in Portland, Oregon that I didn't recognize. The caller identified himself as Barry Mack, a man with whom I had exchanged several emails a few months earlier. He inquired at the time about me doing an interview on an online show that he was helping to promote. His emails stood out in my mind because each one had included a photograph of a striking piece of artwork that he had painted. Each one had a transcendental quality that spoke to me at a soul level.

After we caught up on the progress of the show, I again remarked on how much I enjoyed his style of art. We chatted for a few minutes about the inspiration we both received from tapping into Spirit as we worked.

"I have the sense that beyond the show, there's some way that we can help each other," Barry commented.

"You may be right," I said. "Whoever figures it out first should call the other."

Barry agreed with a laugh and we said our goodbyes.

The next day as Ty and I drove north toward Glacier National Park, my phone rang again. I saw the Portland number and answered, "Hi, Barry."

"Hello, Suzanne," he replied. "I've figured out how you can help me."

"Oh, really?" I said with curiosity. "How's that?"

"You can give me a reading."

When I realized he wasn't kidding, my head fell forward like a dead weight. I truly enjoyed giving readings and felt it was my calling; but my waiting list had grown quite lengthy. I wanted to say yes to everyone who asked for a session, but that just wasn't possible.

"You have someone on the other side you want to connect with?" I asked, hoping he didn't want a reading right away.

"No. I'm in need of some guidance, and I think you're the one who's supposed to give it to me."

Now *I* was the one in need of guidance. I struggled against my immediate reaction, which was to say, *"That's not what I do."*

I had made it a practice to avoid psychic work, which entails tuning in to the personal life of a client and giving him or her advice. I much preferred to connect with loved ones who had passed.

As I paused to find a gentle way to say no, a red-tailed hawk suddenly flashed before my mind's eye. Rather than dismiss the image, I paid attention. I knew that thoughts and images don't simply pop into our minds at random. Quite often they are planted in our consciousness with perfect timing to make a point. I recalled Beth's email and the information she learned about the hawk. As a symbol, it represented higher expressions of psychic work and visions. Could this be Wolf's way of telling me to honor Barry's request, I wondered?

"I'll tell you what," I said. "I have readings lined up all week, so I won't be able to schedule an actual appointment with you. But what if I ask for guidance for you when I meditate, and I'll let you know what I sense?"

"That would be wonderful," Barry replied.

The next day, I found myself with a free half hour with no worries of being interrupted. It was the perfect time to do the psychic experiment.

I connect daily with a special team of helpers in the spirit world. The first time I felt their powerful presence I asked them, "What should I call you?" and they replied, *"You will call us Sanaya, and you should prepare to write, and write, and write as we give you words of wit and wisdom each day."*

When I returned to full waking consciousness, I went to my computer and did a search for "Sanaya." To my amazement, I learned that it was a Sanskrit name that means, "eminent, distinguished, and of the gods." Indeed, since they first made their presence known to me, I have filled notebooks with their messages.

Sananda - Christ consciousness

Sanaya has never failed to give me the perfect answer whenever I had a question that eludes me. I can ask my questions at any time, but I have found that the clearest connection comes when I enter a state of expanded consciousness in meditation. From time to time the vibration I feel from Sanaya changes when new guides come and go as needed. Now I couldn't help but wonder if Wolf had joined the pack and if he would help me as I tried to get a message for the artist, Barry Mack.

I have learned to write out Sanaya's messages in longhand as I hear them. Because Barry's request for guidance was quite general, however, I felt that Sanaya would have more to say than I could keep up with on paper. With tape recorder in hand, I settled on the couch in the coach's living room.

I turned on the recorder and took several slow, deep breaths to release any tension. A tiny voice in my head tried to tell me that I couldn't know anything about a man I had never met. I recognized the voice as that of my ego and agreed with it. I then reminded myself that I didn't need to know anything about Barry because I was about to connect with those who had the answers he desired.

I shifted my consciousness to come into alignment with Sanaya's energy and added a special request for Wolf's help. In this state of communion with Spirit I asked, *"What guidance do you have for Barry Mack?"*

Within seconds my upper left lip twitched, and I relaxed even more. This physiological sign from my guides let me know they were present and ready to get to work.

A concept accompanied by an image came into my mind and I spoke aloud, giving words to the non-verbal impressions. Having crossed this invisible mental barrier, my consciousness blended more fully with Sanaya's and the words began to flow in a slow but steady stream. I focused solely on my role of maintaining the connection without filtering anything through my human mind. I perceived the monologue from afar, my higher self now in the role of Observer.

When I heard the familiar words, *"We bid you goodnight,"* I knew the transmission had ended. I shifted from Observer to Participant and sent a mental *"thank you"* to Sanaya. I slowly counted backwards from ten to one. When my consciousness had returned fully to my body, I opened my eyes and turned off the tape recorder.

I sat still for about a minute, adjusting to my surroundings and enjoying the lingering feeling of serenity that always accompanies a session with Sanaya. I looked down at the tiny screen on the recorder and saw that they had spoken for fifteen minutes. I shook my head, surprised. I felt as if I had closed my eyes only moments earlier.

Still a bit lightheaded, I tried to recall what concepts Sanaya had shared. Their message included the kind of intimate issues a counselor might take multiple sessions to uncover. I remembered hearing something during the transmission about a fox totem as it related to an issue in Barry's life. I had no idea what the fox as a sacred symbol represents or if Barry was dealing with the issue Sanaya specified.

I felt a flurry of excitement. The fact that an animal totem came up in the session showed me that Wolf had participated as part of the group. Sanaya had never mentioned totems in any sessions before Wolf entered my life.

A part of me wanted to listen to the recording, but I knew that only one person needed to judge its contents. I pulled my computer onto my lap from beside me on the couch and plugged the digital recorder into a USB port. As the file uploaded I composed an email to Barry.

"Attached is a recording of the guidance I just received for you from Spirit," I wrote him. "I have not listened to it, but I trust it will speak to you. I look forward to hearing your thoughts and hope you find the messages helpful."

I hit "send" and sat back, feeling a bit nervous, yet excited about doing my first purely psychic session with no feedback. I had just taken a leap of faith into oceans where few former naval officers ever ventured or knew much about. The landing would be hard or soft, depending on Barry's feedback.

I checked my inbox frequently until bedtime, but received no emails from Barry Mack. The next morning Ty and I got on the road early. The cell phone signal was intermittent as we traveled north toward Kalispell, Montana. Two hours into the trip I was able to log in to my email account and smiled when I saw an email from BarryMackArt, the name of his artistic blog.

I held my breath as I opened the message. Had the visionary powers of the hawk truly accompanied me during my fledgling flight? Barry's opening words put me instantly at ease.

"Thank you, Suzanne and Sanaya," he wrote. "Your message was perfect in every way and was exactly what I needed to hear. The recorded message is one of the great highlights of my life. Listening to it brought a flood of tears because I feel the truth and rejoice in its wisdom."

It was I who wanted to weep as I felt the effects of Sanaya's words on a fellow soul. Barry apologized for expressing his thanks through an impersonal email, but he realized that I was most likely out of cell phone range. While I would have enjoyed the personal connection, I appreciated being able to savor his written remarks.

I read on and shook my head when Barry offered to thank me materially for my help. We hadn't discussed a fee for the session, and I had no plans to ask for compensation. I wasn't surprised that he would offer some kind of thank you, but I was stunned when I read what he had in mind.

"I would like to offer you the painting below as a gift," Barry wrote.

Just as in his previous emails, he had inserted a photo of one of his paintings at the bottom of the message. Like his other works of art, this one drew me in, instantly transporting me to another world with its sweeping lines. His skillful use of light made the heavenly scene glow with life.

My heart beat more rapidly as I returned to the text of the email. "It is 48 inches high by 60 inches wide. If it's too large, I have some images to choose from, and can send a smaller print. I understand if you don't feel it's necessary, but this is a pivotal moment, perhaps the most important moment in my life. So naturally, I feel a desire to thank you with all my heart."

Over the past few years of helping to connect people with their loved ones who had passed, I had received many heartfelt thanks. I knew that the evidence I brought through from the spirit world changed lives, but this was the first time that providing personal guidance had impacted someone to such an extent. I sent waves of gratitude to my team of helpers who had brought such healing to Barry.

I returned my gaze to the bottom of the email and studied the painting more closely. The thumbnail image was indeed captivating. I could only imagine how stunning it would be in its full four-foot by five-foot glory. Not only was the painting the perfect size for the wall above the couch in my study at home, but the colors matched those in my study. It was as if Barry had selected them with that room in mind.

I had been searching for an inspiring piece of art to hang above the sofa in the room where I gave my readings. The framed photo of a lighthouse that currently occupied the space was eye-catching, but I wanted something that resonated with the sacred energy I tapped into on a regular basis in my special sanctuary.

If I had seen the painting in a gallery, I felt sure that I would have longingly admired it, but such a stunning piece would not normally fit into our budget. I fully intended to tell Barry that I could not accept his offer. It was simply too generous of a gift in exchange for a fifteen minute psychic session. Thanks to Sanaya, the effort on my part had seemed effortless. I could only imagine the time, effort, and expense that Barry had put into this piece, along with a piece of his soul.

I was about to compose my reply, when I realized that I hadn't finished reading his email. I shifted my gaze back to where I had become distracted by the painting.

"It's an amazing message," he wrote about the contents of the recording. "It is absolutely right on. You really should listen to it. There is no doubt you connected with higher consciousness."

I smiled with gratitude. I always found this kind of confirmation encouraging. Still, I didn't feel that my contribution equaled the value of his painting until I came to the end of the email. There, with one simple question he revealed why he felt the need to gift me with such a precious treasure: "How do you thank one properly," he wrote, "for saving your life?"

I stared at the screen, dumbfounded. He was right. I did need to listen to the recording. Whatever Sanaya said had been far more meaningful than the bits and pieces that I heard during the transmission. I realized then that there were certain things in life that we can't put a price on, whether they be a fine piece of art or a life-changing message. I felt immensely humbled to serve as the conduit for a message that carried such profound healing. I knew now that I could accept his gift with gratitude and humility. Its presence in my study would serve as an ongoing reminder of the transformative power of my work.

I called Barry later that day. We immediately launched into a discussion of the information that had come through from Sanaya. Even though his email had confirmed the reading's accuracy, I felt a thrill when I heard the specifics of each issue. One item in particular prompted me to share what I learned after listening to the recording.

"Do you remember when Sanaya spoke about the fox being your totem?" I asked.

"Yes," he said. "I've listened to the recording several times now. I am familiar with every word."

"I went on the Internet and looked up the fox as a sacred symbol," I told him. "When the fox appears in your life, you need to pay attention to people or situations that may be taking you down a path that doesn't serve you. The fox warns you to be more discerning at a time when you may be cunningly led to do something you might not normally do."

"That's exactly what Sanaya was talking about in the part of the message where the subject of the fox came up," Barry said.

"I know," I said, thrilled at the validation. "I've never had a fox come up in a session before."

I then shared with Barry that the mention of a totem in his reading carried an important message for me, as well. It validated that I had a new member on my team of helpers.

"So we really were meant to help each other," he said.

"Yes," I said, grateful that I had agreed to do the reading. "But I think you should take some time and make sure you really want to part with such a beautiful painting."

"I don't need to think it over," he said. "I already feel like a completely different person. Sanaya's message to have faith and believe in our own magnificence is so important. This is transformation at its best."

I knew he spoke the truth. I could feel the increase in his vibration from the last time we spoke. His offer truly came from the heart, and I thanked him again. We chatted for a few minutes about the logistics of shipping the painting from Oregon to Florida.

"I can't tell you how excited I am about having one of your paintings in the room where I meditate and give my readings," I said. "It has such an ethereal quality to it."

"I'm in an altered state when I paint," Barry said, confirming what I already suspected. "My work is a glimpse into a higher world."

"I can feel that," I replied. "Do you have a name for this one?"

The question was innocent enough, so I was ill-prepared for the shock of Barry's answer.

"I call it 'Going Home.'"

If I harbored any doubts that Wolf played a part in Barry's reading, they vanished in that instant.

"It was like going home to draw these things," Wolf had said in his initial reading. "Going Home," echoed Barry Mack's painting.

Both Wolf Pasakarnis and Barry Mack were artists, but like yin and yang, their styles were at opposite ends of the spectrum. One drew primitive sketches, the other painted museum-quality masterpieces. Their inspiration, however, came from the same Source.

I thought about the hawk that Wolf had shown me from his eternal home. That symbol of greater visionary power led me to receive a gift more valuable than the priceless work of art that would soon grace the walls of my physical home. I was gifted with a greater view across the veil—a veil that bit by bit was turning out to be more transparent than I had imagined.

CHAPTER ELEVEN

Gifts

The three-way phone call during which I told Mike and Beth about Barry Mack's reading is one that stands out from the many special conversations we shared as our spiritual journey with Wolf unfolded.

"My son helped to save someone's life?" Mike asked in a tone of wonder.

"Yes," I replied. "He was part of a group of spirit guides who brought the information through. I wouldn't have done the reading if Wolf hadn't shown me the hawk the first time he visited me."

"Tell her what we found yesterday," Beth urged Mike.

"Something about Wolf?" I asked, intrigued.

"I was going to call you, but you beat me to it," Mike said. "You're not going to believe this."

One thing I had learned during the past few years was to be open-minded. So, with eager anticipation I said, "Try me."

Mike paused for a moment before explaining. "I was out in the yard last night. When I walked by Wolf's old bedroom, I noticed a smear on the window that wasn't there before."

I furrowed my brow, trying to imagine where this was leading.

"I looked down on the ground and couldn't believe my eyes," Mike continued. "There was a dead bird in the grass right under Wolf's window."

I blinked in astonishment. "Under *Wolf's* window?" I asked to verify I had heard correctly.

"Yep."

The left side of my brain immediately tried to rationalize the situation. Birds fly into windows. It's rare, but it happens. The probability of a bird flying directly into Wolf's bedroom window, however, was so remote that the mention of it in his initial visit to me now deserved to be rated a "super hit."

"Did you happen to take a picture of it?" I asked.

"I sure did."

"He called me over as soon as he saw the bird," Beth put in. "We immediately understood the significance of it. The picture shows the bird and the window with the smear in the same shot."

My fingers curled into tight fists. This was evidence of life beyond death of the highest quality. It served as an excellent reminder not to become discouraged when something in a reading doesn't make sense right away. What puzzled me was the timing of the bird's demise. I had assumed that when Wolf showed me the image, it referred to a past event, but Mike and Beth had no specific memory of any such incident involving Wolf. It never dawned on me that Wolf was referring to something that would occur in the future.

I reminded myself that time in the spirit world does not unfold in linear fashion as it does in our physical world. Those on the other side often remind me that from their perspective it is only a blink of an eye until they are reunited with those they left behind. Nevertheless, I had to marvel at the bird's-eye view that allowed Wolf to foresee an event three weeks before it occurred.

Mike and Beth were equally amazed at how the things Wolf had shared in his reading were now coming to light one by one. When we said goodbye to each other, we suffered few doubts that from the way things were evolving, we would be talking again soon.

I was still pondering the nature of time the next day as Ty and I wandered around Depot Park in Whitefish, Montana. We were fortunate to arrive on a Tuesday, perfect timing to enjoy the weekly farmer's market held there during the summer months. We had visited my nephew Matthew and his wife Eleanor at their Whitefish home two years earlier, but our timing then didn't allow us access to the festive atmosphere of the market.

I couldn't believe how the past two years had changed Matthew's family. Their daughter, Olive, could barely walk the last time we visited. Today she danced in circles on the park's soft grass in perfect rhythm with a live band entertaining the crowd. I marveled at little Ruthie nestled in Eleanor's arms. Her beautiful soul had not yet begun its earthly existence on our previous visit. Now here she was, gracing us with her presence, her large eyes filled with wonder as she took in the stimulating scents, sights, and sounds of the market. When both of my great-nieces began to wind down at the same time, we made plans to meet the next day.

Ty and I retrieved our bicycles and began pedaling back to the coach. As we approached one of the main intersections in the small mountain town, I flashed back to our previous visit. I remembered being pleasantly surprised to find a metaphysical shop a short way down the street from where we were now waiting at a traffic light.

Just like the experience one week earlier when I passed the Barnes and Noble store in my hometown, I felt a magnetic pull in the direction of the store. When I shared this with Ty, he rolled his eyes and smiled.

"What?" I said, with feigned indignity. "There's something there for me. I can feel it."

"That's a good line, Suzanne," he said with the good-natured laugh I had long become accustomed to. "You go ahead and I'll see you back at the coach."

As he pedaled away, I headed down East Street. Under normal circumstances I might wonder if the store were still there, but the insistent pull assured me it was. Sure enough, after two short blocks I pulled up under the sign for "Rocks and Things" and secured my bike against a light pole.

I walked into the shop and breathed in the distinctive aromas emitted by various candles, essential oils, and exotic incense, the blend of which produced a perfume unique to this kind of store. I knew from prior experience that the scent would permeate my clothes and linger on them long after I left.

I glanced at the only other customer, a young man with jet-black hair that fell past his shoulders. He wore a full-length trench coat covered with large, white, hand-painted spirals. My eyes widened, but I did my best to simply observe without being judgmental. My current work had taken me a considerable distance from my days at the Pentagon.

I turned to the left and began a slow clockwise tour of the store's display cases. I had no idea what I was searching for, so I simply allowed my eyes to linger for a few moments on each object. I willed something to move as the book at Barnes and Noble had, but nothing moved or spoke to me in that or any other way.

I noticed some motion to my right and turned to see a woman with long, straight hair emerge from behind a curtain. From my previous visit I recognized her as the owner of the shop. Our eyes met, and we both smiled.

"I remember you," she said with a slight tilt of her head.

"I remember you, too," I replied with a nod. "You have quite a good memory. It's been two years since I was here last."

I apologized for not remembering her name, and she re-introduced herself as Velvet.

"Can I help you find something?" she asked.

I shook my head and told her that I just wanted to look around. In truth, I knew that I didn't need or want anything, but I couldn't shake the feeling that there was something "in store" for me there. I continued working my way around the display cases. Several times I glanced at Velvet and caught her watching me. Each time that happened, we locked eyes for a moment before looking away.

I made a complete circuit of the store while Velvet helped the young man in the trench coat. Nothing I looked at jumped out at me either literally or figuratively. The need to be there did not fade, however, so I began a second round, this time in search of something I might have missed on the first round. When I returned to the entrance, I once again noticed Velvet watching me. I held her gaze for an awkward moment, wondering what might be the strange attraction we obviously shared with each other.

I stood in the entryway, still empty-handed, unwilling to leave without discovering the reason why I had been drawn to this store. I was reading some flyers and business cards posted on the wall by the door when Velvet approached me.

"I don't know why I'm saying this," she said, "but do you want to get together and talk?"

I laughed shyly. Under other circumstances, I might have interpreted the question as some sort of come-on, but I knew that wasn't how she meant it. In one simple sentence, I summed up the sense of understanding that now enveloped me.

"We're *supposed* to talk," I said.

"I know," she replied matter-of-factly.

We gave each other a small but sincere smile. Standing in the foyer of her store, neither of us knew why we felt the need to chat, but we both understood at a soul level that higher forces were calling us together.

"I'll tell you what," I said. "Tomorrow is my birthday. For the past four years, Spirit has given me some incredible gifts on my birthday. I have a feeling that you're part of this year's gift, so why don't we get together tomorrow morning for coffee?"

She agreed, and we arranged to meet at a crepe shop around the corner.

I turned to leave and realized with a start that the urge to be in her store had vanished. Just like that it was gone, in company with my frustration. In its place, I was filled with the realization that I had been drawn there not for some *thing*, but for some *one*.

The next morning at ten o'clock I arrived at Amazing Crepes. As I had already eaten breakfast, I bought a simple cup of decaffeinated coffee. I knew that Velvet and I would likely be discussing topics that might raise an eyebrow or two, so I chose the table that offered the most privacy.

When Velvet arrived, she declined anything to eat or drink and took the seat across from me.

"Happy Birthday," she said kindly.

"Thanks," I replied, pleased that she remembered.

We looked at each other, each of us waiting for the other to speak first.

Finally Velvet spoke. "I don't know what we're supposed to talk about."

And we shared a chuckle.

I took a sip of coffee and felt myself relaxing in the presence of a kindred spirit. We clearly both understood the peace that comes from trusting our inner guidance.

"You know," I said, after searching my mind for the reason we had been brought together, "I think I'm supposed to tell you about this fellow named Wolf who's been coming to me from the other side."

Velvet nodded, and I started at the beginning. I told her about meeting Mike and Beth at the A.R.E. conference in Virginia Beach. I shared that our children were both killed by a lightning strike and that both of them had left signs of their impending death. I finished the preamble by describing Wolf's prophetic poem and the drawing he made of the tree with two roses at its base.

All others with whom I had shared the story to that point had responded with wonder upon hearing the details. Velvet merely nodded, as if she took events of this magnitude as a matter of course.

"Do you know what this is?" she asked, as she touched an object hanging from a chain around her neck.

I studied the strange object that resembled a petrified piece of penne pasta with lengthwise grooves on the outside. Gray and rough, it was not the sort of thing one would normally wear on a necklace.

"I have no idea," I replied.

"It's a fulgurite," Velvet said.

I shrugged my shoulders. "What is that?"

"A fulgurite," she intoned, "is sand that forms into a tubular shaped crystal when it's struck by lightning."

"You're kidding," I said, leaning in now for a closer look.

Velvet explained that the crystal is a powerful metaphysical tool, believed to enhance the powers of one's prayers because it harnesses the mighty power of the force that created it.

"Would you like to have it?" she asked.

I sat back and stared at the necklace as I sorted through the mix of emotions her offer evoked. For a long while after Susan was killed by lightning, I panicked whenever an electrical storm erupted. I would also turn away from pictures of lightning bolts or other reminders of her tragic passing. My perception of death completely changed, however, as I awakened to the existence of a greater reality. Now, I found myself strangely drawn to this tangible reminder of the power of Nature, which, like death, no longer frightens me.

"You would give that to me?" I asked, stunned that she would offer to part with such a rare treasure.

In a telling display of one who grasps what is truly important in this life, Velvet reached behind her neck and unclasped the necklace. "I have no attachment to things," she said as she handed it to me.

I thanked her as best I could and placed the crystal in my purse. We continued talking about Wolf and the signs he left behind. When I mentioned the yin-yang symbol in his final drawing, Velvet again nodded in understanding.

"He came to you because part of your mission is to help restore balance in the masculine and feminine energies," she said. "Two eyes represent duality, but the single eye represents seeing with neutrality and compassion. The eye of God is the heart."

"That gives me goose bumps," I said, rubbing my arms.

Velvet smiled. "I call them 'truth shivers.'"

"I love that!" I exclaimed and pulled a notepad from my purse to record those words to memory.

We then shifted our discussion to talking about Velvet's work. She shared that she had recently completed certification as an instructor of kundalini yoga, a form unfamiliar to me. I listened intently as she described a practice that combines meditation, breathing, and various postures to increase spiritual awareness.

I silently wished that Ty and I could remain longer in Whitefish. I would have loved to study with Velvet, whose energy I found peaceful and soothing. Unfortunately, Ty and I had reservations the following week in Banff and Lake Louise, three hundred miles to the north.

She then began to share with me a special mission she had been led to carry out. In a series of downloads from her guides, she was told to leave crystals in various places throughout the Rocky Mountains. "It's a way of restoring the crystalline grid around the planet," she said, describing this grid as Earth's original blueprint.

Well aware of how strange our conversation might sound to those unfamiliar with metaphysics, I was secretly relieved that I had chosen a table out of earshot of the other customers. I too would have looked askance at talk of crystalline grids and downloads from spirit guides had it not been for an incident that happened on my birthday two years earlier ...

I had returned to the coach that night from my annual trip home to visit my mother. I awoke at 2:30 and felt an unusual sensation in my body, as if I were being shaken back and forth by an unseen hand. Geometric shapes and algebraic-type numbers flew past my mind's eye as a voice advised me to "just go with it."

I rolled onto my side, picked up my pen, and wrote the phrases that followed exactly as I heard then in the dark:

Crystals are most beneficial
Interstellar communications
Informational transmission is compromised when the grid is compromised. Yours is now optimized for maximum attunement.
See the honeycomb. See the patterns.
Digital ... binary codes. 1's and 2's, on and off ...
Crop circle geometry is in code. See the stellated dodecahedron.

When I heard the latter two words I drew two asterisks after them and wrote on in the dark of night as the download continued. It ended with:

Here now to bring teachings of love
The stellated dodecahedron will bring recognition.

I was intrigued by this unusual transmission. It was quite different from most of Sanaya's poetic messages, but I was too sleepy to give the words much thought at the time. I awoke the next morning with only a vague memory of having received a download in the middle of the night. Were it not for the crooked lines of writing on the notepad by my pillow, I might have dismissed it as a dream.

When I reviewed the notes, I was struck by the technical nature of the information and recalled the geometric and mathematical images I had seen in my mind's eye. None of the notes made any sense to me, most especially the term "stellated dodecahedron." I knew with an absolute certainty that I had never seen or heard the term before and because I hadn't, it could not have come from either my conscious or subconscious mind.

As I sat on the edge of the bed wondering if such a thing as a stellated dodecahedron existed, a loud, clear voice said, *"Look in the purple book."*

I shook my head to make sure I hadn't imagined the voice, even though there was no mistaking the command. A stack of five new books stood on the nightstand. I bought them while home in Florida and I had brought them back with me to read during the rest of our trip. I had not read any of them yet. The third book from the bottom had a purple cover. I stared at it, almost afraid to look in the index.

If "stellated dodecahedron" is in there, I thought, *I am not going to know how to handle this.*

I pulled the book from the stack and turned to the index in the back. I scanned the columns until I came to the S's. When my gaze fell on the very two words I had heard in the darkness, I laid the book in my lap and lowered my head, as if in prayer. I may not have known intellectually how to handle this stunning discovery, but my body responded with very real tears that flowed down my cheeks. This clarity of reception represented a level of attunement with higher consciousness that until that moment was something I had only dreamed of.

When I turned to the page in the book indicated by the index, I learned that a stellated dodecahedron is the geometrical shape of an energetic grid that allegedly surrounds the Earth. Also known as the "Christ consciousness" or "unity consciousness" grid, it holds the pattern for our physical planet. A black and white diagram in the book showed a polyhedron with twelve faces with five pentagrams meeting at each vertex. Next to this diagram was the same shape superimposed over the Earth.

I was keenly aware that no scientific evidence exists to validate any of this theoretical information. I also knew that much of my work as a medium cannot yet be validated by science, but that does not make the evidence I receive from the spirit world any less real. To receive a transmission of "stellated dodecahedron" and be led directly to its reference in a book that I had not yet read, made me want to learn more about this alleged grid.

I immediately sat to meditate and asked Sanaya for further guidance. When I slipped into a more expanded state of consciousness, I was shown a grid around our planet much like the one depicted in the book, only this grid was incomplete. Then flashing before my mind's eye was an image of a satellite photograph of the Earth taken at night. The picture showed much of the planet in darkness, with concentrations of light in populated areas. I understood that Sanaya was making an analogy between the actual physical lights as seen from space and the light that burns within each human heart.

Sanaya explained that human beings are made of energy, as is the Earth. All energy is connected. Therefore, how we think and act affects the consciousness of not just the people on the Earth, but the Earth itself. Just as there are large areas of physical darkness around our planet, there are large concentrations of spiritual darkness as well, resulting in gaps in the energetic grid.

I scribbled notes with my eyes closed as Sanaya continued with the lesson. They showed me that as people come into alignment with their true self and become heart-centered, they achieve a state known as "Christ consciousness" or "unity consciousness." Sanaya reminded me that the term has nothing to do with whether or not one is a Christian or holds any other religious beliefs. It describes a state in which a person realizes that we are all one with our Source, with God. When an individual turns up the light inside and becomes aware of his or her own divinity, one more light in the Christ consciousness grid turns on.

Having learned this lesson from my guides exactly two years earlier, I didn't laugh when Velvet described her mission to strengthen the grid by placing crystals along the spine of the Earth. I pictured the final image Sanaya had shared with me that memorable morning in which I heard with new ears and saw with new eyes. They showed me their vision of a fully activated grid in the form of a sparkling stellated dodecahedron surrounding our beautiful, living planet.

When I asked Velvet how her mission was progressing, she told me that she had realized most of it.

"I only have one more crystal left to put in place," she said.

"Where's that?" I asked.

"In Lake Louise."

Now I did laugh. I laughed aloud from the sheer joy of yet another wondrous "coincidence."

She cocked her head in question, waiting for me to tell her what she had said that I found so amusing.

"Lake Louise is the next stop on our trip," I informed her.

Instead of laughing with me, Velvet smiled and slowly nodded her head at the perfection of the timing. When I offered to take a crystal to Lake Louise for her, she surprised me by saying yes. I realized that it didn't matter who placed the crystal, only that the mission be fulfilled.

"I'm not planning to go to Canada any time soon," she said, "even though it's beautiful in Banff National Park."

"We've never been there, but I've heard the scenery is amazing."

"You're going to love it," she said. "You probably know that Banff and Lake Louise are associated with the energy of Archangel Michael."

I jerked my head with a start. I didn't know anything about an alleged connection between Banff and Archangel Michael. Until a few years earlier I also didn't know about crystalline grids, geometric shapes with tongue-twisting names, or efforts to seed crystals around the planet. I did not foresee birds flying into windows with the precision of a guided missile, nor did I contemplate an association with two Michaels whose powerful energy left me shaking.

The worldview I had clung to for most of my life had been shaken so greatly that I couldn't help but let it dissolve, bit by bit. Now, thanks to this unexpected meeting with an old soul with energy as soft as velvet, I was being asked to stretch my belief system yet again. I took a final sip of coffee and thanked my new friend for the gift. She and I both knew that I was referring to much more than just the fulgurite in my purse.

I left the crepe shop and headed for the coach with my head swimming. I could hardly wait to get to Lake Louise.

CHAPTER TWELVE

One Big Web

The campground in Banff lies several miles up a substantial hill from the downtown area. The fastest route there from the Trans-Canada Highway is via the Banff Avenue exit south of town. At the left turn onto Tunnel Mountain Road a bright yellow sign proclaims in large, bold letters, "Attention! Wildlife crossing next 3 kilometers." A drawing beneath the words depicts three animals walking in single-file: a large elk with a full rack of antlers, a hump-backed grizzly bear, and a sleek, gray wolf. As we made the left turn past the sign, I thought how marvelous it would be to see a wolf in the wild. I wasn't so sure about the grizzly bear.

We passed the sign several times during our visit to Banff as we drove to the various trailheads throughout the area. The Honda CRV that we towed behind the coach was the perfect vehicle for exploring the mountain roads. Now on our drive home from an invigorating hike near the scenic Vermillion Lakes, my body hummed from having spent the afternoon outdoors in the rugged wild. At no time did I feel more alive and attuned than when immersed in the glory of Nature, and the Canadian Rockies carried some of the best-feeling energy in North America. In every direction one sees craggy peaks jutting skyward at odd angles, seemingly scraping the clouds with their razor-toothed edges. The views available to us as we returned to the coach would have been spectacular were it not for a line of ominous black clouds bearing down on us.

"We're going to get back just in time," I said, casting a weather eye on the gathering storm.

"We may," Ty agreed, "but I don't think that jogger's going to make it."

I glanced ahead and saw a lone woman half a mile ahead of us running in the same direction as we were driving. We had traveled the road enough times since our arrival in Banff to know that the nearest shelter lay at least two miles ahead.

In wordless agreement, Ty slowed the car and I rolled down the window as we drew alongside the young woman.

"You're about to get soaked," I said and pointed at the clouds approaching from behind. "Would you like a ride? It's a long way to wherever you're going."

She shook her head and continued running. "No, thanks. I'm fine."

Ty ducked his head down to see her and asked, "Are you sure?"

"Yes, thank you anyway," she said and waved us off.

I glanced at Ty and threw up my hands in disbelief. At least we had tried.

Five minutes later, just as we pulled up to the coach, the storm's fury hit, dropping the temperature twenty degrees in as many seconds, pummeling the campground with rain, and bending over the tall trees in savage shrieks of wind. Sitting in the car, I shuddered as I pictured the jogger somewhere behind us on the exposed roadway.

Ty and I had jogged enough times in the rain to know that it can be perversely fun to dodge raindrops. We would not have been concerned for the girl had it not been for the grumble of thunder and daggers of lightning that accentuated the downpour. We shared a knowing glance.

"I'm going back," I said.

"Good," my husband replied, "I'll take care of the puppies." He opened the door of the car and made a dash for the coach, where our dogs had been cooped up since we left for our hike.

I shifted position to behind the wheel as best I could and made my way back along the route we had just traveled. The windshield wipers slapped furiously back and forth. When I came upon the girl I made a quick U-turn and pulled alongside her.

"Please get in," I begged through the rolled down passenger window.

This time she relented. "I'm going to get your car all wet," she apologized even as she slid onto the front seat.

"It will dry," I said. "It's not safe to be out there with lightning around."

"Oh, that's not a problem," she said. "It's just a lot colder than I was expecting."

I rolled up the electric window as she buckled her seat belt and we headed toward the town. I drew in a breath as a flash of lightning fired up the sky.

"Actually, storms are a bigger problem than most people realize," I informed her in no uncertain terms. "My step-daughter was just about your age when she was struck and killed by lightning."

I glanced over to make sure my words registered with my young guest. When I saw her eyes widen I added, "And I'm in touch with the family of another young man who was killed the same way."

"I'm so sorry," she said.

"Thousands of people are struck by lightning each year," I explained further. "My husband and I didn't want you to become a statistic."

I dropped her off at an apartment complex just down the hill from the campground, and she thanked me for the ride. As I headed back to the coach, I wondered if I had averted a tragedy. One part of me knew that if it were time for the young woman's soul to return home, it would find some other way to do so. The other side of me thanked God that her family would not suffer heartache on that day.

By the next morning the clouds had cleared and the sun was sparkling on the peaks of Mt. Rundle across from our campsite. While Ty took the dogs for a walk, I moved a kitchen chair into the bedroom and closed the door. I gathered my notepad and pen and sat down to meditate. After sending prayers of gratitude I enjoyed a period of sitting in the silence, happy to spend this sacred period of communion with Spirit. About ten minutes into the session my right index finger twitched. Recognizing the familiar sign, I picked up my pen and prepared to take dictation.

I had followed this special ritual religiously for four years. Each day I receive a message meant not just for me, but for those led to read Sanaya's inspiring communications on my blog or Facebook page. I never choose the topic, and Sanaya never lacks for words, often using clever analogies to offer a unique twist to universal truths.

Poised to write, I willed all conscious thought to drift away. And then, from the void I heard a most unexpected word.

"Snowshoes."

"Snowshoes?" I echoed back in my mind. *"Are you serious? It's August."*

"Write it down," they said, and I dutifully did so. I might question my team of helpers, but I rarely argued for long.

Once I surrendered and set my pen in motion, the words flowed with ease:

Snowshoes ... they keep you from sinking into soft snow as you walk. Because of the shape, it makes the snow seem solid. Were it not for the large footprint, you would blend into the snow. And so it is with the body. Were it not for your physical "footprint," you would blend in with the molecules of the Earth. See the physical world as it truly is today, not as your senses report it to be. All is a buzzing hive of vibration. As such, the physical world is an illusion. Take away the physical senses, and what you are left with is vibration itself, arising from pure consciousness. Love is the impulse from which all arises and forms. Take away all extraneous things, and all that remains is Love. Simply reflect on this and see how it changes things for you.

When the message ended, I thanked Sanaya and brought myself back to full waking consciousness. Moving from the bedroom to the living room, I typed the hand-written phrases in a Word document on my laptop. Normally I would connect to the Internet and post the message to my blog. Unfortunately, we had no Internet signal in the national park. The nearest hotspot was at a youth hostel a hundred yards away.

With the document saved, I turned off the computer, slipped it into a tote bag, and headed for the door, passing Ty and the pups on my way out of the coach.

"I'm off to the hostel to update the blog," I announced. "I'll only be a few minutes."

"Okay," he said, "I'll have breakfast ready when you get back, and then we'll pack up to head for Lake Louise."

"Sounds good," I called over my shoulder.

I walked fifty yards down the road and stopped to allow one of the local buses to pass. The first time I saw one of them drive through the campground, I ran back to the coach to grab my camera. Although it was highly unusual to provide public transportation in a campground, that wasn't what had me shaking my head in wonder. Rather, it was the pack of life-sized gray wolves pictured on the side and back of all of the local buses. Everywhere I went in Banff I saw these wolves. Even while sitting at our kitchen table or looking out the windows from the couch I saw the wolves ride by on their regularly scheduled run through the park.

After the bus went by, I crossed the road and stepped through an opening in a fence that marked the perimeter of the campground. Now on the grounds of the hostel, I cut across a patch of grass until I came to a walkway leading to the front of the inn. Each time I used the Internet while in Banff I followed the same path, and each time when I arrived at the hostel's main entrance I sent Wolf a silent greeting. As if the wolves weren't enough to remind me of his presence, a poster taped to the glass door brought him fully to mind.

"*Great music throughout July and August*" the colorful banner announced across the top. Below was a list of musical entertainment the city had lined up for the short summer season. I had never heard of any of the five bands listed. One of them, however, stood out from the rest, and I was sorry I had missed hearing the group's performance. The same week that I was at home in Florida reading *Twilight of the Gods*, the tourists in Banff were being entertained by none other than the Australian rock band, *Pacha Mamma.*

I walked into the hostel and connected to its Internet signal. After posting Sanaya's message and checking email, I went back to find Ty already hooking up our Honda to the tow hitch at the back of the coach. After a quick breakfast we broke camp and motored thirty miles north to Lake Louise. Our campsite there rivaled the one in Banff. Through the front windshield we enjoyed an unobstructed view of massive Mt. Temple sporting a glistening glacier draped across its broad shoulders like a thick white scarf. At ground level, close by our coach, a rushing river carried blue-green snowmelt down past its rocky banks.

After dinner that evening I was sitting on the couch reading a book when Ty suddenly pointed out the front window and shouted, "Grizzlies!" Rudy and Gretchen began barking furiously, not because they saw the bears, but in response to Ty's excited outburst. Leaving the dogs in the safety of the coach, Ty rushed outside armed with his Nikon. I followed close behind with a canister of bear spray, the land equivalent of shark repellent.

Keeping to the road, we walked cautiously in the direction the bears had gone. When we saw some fellow campers pointing toward the river, we joined the huddle and peered into the trees. No more than a hundred feet away stood two 250-pound grizzlies. Too young to know any better, they stared back at us with equal curiosity, providing the perfect pose for some of the most memorable photos of our summer tour.

The next morning I awoke with a feeling of excitement even greater than when I saw the bears. This was the day I planned to take Velvet's crystal to Lake Louise. Before I did, however, I needed to spend some time with my team in spirit.

While Ty took the pups outside, I retreated to the bedroom to meditate. As always, I expressed my gratitude and then enjoyed an extended period of sitting in the silence. About the time that I would normally receive a message from Sanaya, a wolf's face unexpectedly appeared before my mind's eye. Startled, I jerked, but willed myself to relax and remain receptive. Moments later I heard two phrases and instinctively wrote them down:

Now you see
What it means to be free . . .

As soon as I felt the lilting cadence and heard the rhyme, I sent a silent *thank you*. The first full year of messages received from Spirit were transmitted to me in the form of poetry. Most of the inspiration I had received from Sanaya in the three years since was in the form of prose. It had been quite a while since they had sent me a poem, and I missed the beautiful verses. I pictured the wolf's face I had seen in my mind's eye and wondered if Wolf himself was being helped by my team this morning. I recalled that the poetry he had left behind did not normally rhyme, but I recognized his influence in the subject matter. Any mention of freedom harkened to the wolf's core being.

Having written the first two lines, a torrent of words followed as quickly as I could copy them onto my notepad:

No longer encumbered
As the one who still slumbered
But awakened to who and what you are
You had no need to go far
For the answers were there
Hidden in plain sight
They came to you at night
When you wrote without a light

99

And will continue now apace
As you see the wolf's strong face
He brings you guidance, as you asked
With this job he has been tasked
For it's all a great big web
Which is what has oft been said
When you see the strands you know
This is how you're supposed to grow
Just relax now, settle back
As your desires you attack
And the ego you release
This is the road to peace

When the transmission ended, I laid my pen down and opened my eyes. I lifted the notepad from my lap and read the words with an overwhelming sense of awe. When I got to the end I shook my head, struck by the meaningful message. I recognized in the last three lines the Buddhist philosophy of non-attachment: *As your desires you attack and the ego you release, this is the road to peace.*

So that's what he meant by freedom, I thought. I pictured the many drawings Wolf left behind of a heart with chains across it. They expressed in visual form his recurring theme of freedom. I recalled also his final poem which read like a prayer:

Spirit of Great Healer, awaken from within this heart.
Peace and tranquility flow like water.
The time has come to allow the light of nature to free my soul.

Is this why you continue to come to me? I asked Wolf. *Is it to teach others to attain the peace and freedom you struggled so hard to find?*

I thought of my recent conversation with Velvet in Montana when we discussed the yin-yang symbol that Wolf also included in so many of his works. She had sensed that Wolf came to me as part of a mutual mission to help create balance in our world.

I understand about having a sense of mission. It was an integral part of my military training and it has stayed with me even though I no longer wear a uniform. After Susan passed and I discovered that I as a medium can connect with those who had crossed over to the spirit world, I made it my mission to share the messages of hope with as many people as possible. That mission had expanded to encompass a broad range of spiritual topics. I couldn't help but wonder if my mission was taking on a new focus with Wolf's spirit at my side.

The assumption seemed valid when I reread the poem: *The answers will continue now apace as you see the Wolf's strong face. He brings you guidance, as you asked. With this job he has been tasked.*

I welcome your teachings, I said as I sent Wolf a wave of gratitude. *We need them.*

In response, he drew my attention back to his poem and the words *"for it's all a great big web."* As I reread them, the image of the eye from his final drawing appeared in my mind. In the center I saw the familiar yin-yang symbol. The tree with the red roses stood out on the right.

Look on the left side, he urged me now.

When I tried to see the image more closely, it faded from view like a wispy dream. Frustrated, I went to the living room and turned on my laptop. I opened the folder with the files I had saved about Wolf and pulled up the photograph of his final drawing.

As directed, I looked at the left side of the large eye. It was more densely filled in than the right side or the center. I recalled asking Mike and Beth when they first showed me the drawing if the squiggly lines on the left had any meaning. Beth told me it was a picture of a dream catcher. I didn't think anything of it at the time. I was more interested in the yin-yang symbol and the two red roses.

As I studied the left side more closely, I clearly saw what I had missed before. What at first glance appeared to be haphazard lines was actually a circle with a grid inside it. Four squiggly feathers hung from the bottom of the circle. I pursed my lips as I continued studying the sketch. I knew nothing about the history or purpose of dream catchers. In fact, I realized with a start, the only person I knew who had ever owned a dream catcher was my step-daughter, Susan.

A sudden urge to learn more about dream catchers spurred me to open a web browser. I typed the words *"meaning of dream catchers"* in the search box and hit the "enter" key. A full page of results appeared on the screen along with thumbnail images of dream catchers that emulated Wolf's crude drawing.

I shook my head in amazement when I saw the top result. It read, *"History of the Dream Catchers – the Wolf's Den Creations."* I clicked on the URL and found myself staring at a wolf's face not unlike the one in my mind's eye that had preceded the morning's visit.

A quick read of the site's homepage informed me that Native Americans believe dreams are messages sent by spirits. A dream catcher placed by a bed will catch bad dreams in its webbing. Good dreams are allowed to slip through a hole in the middle of the web.

Even though the site had not been updated since 2005, it included a timeless quote by Chief Seattle, the legendary leader of the Duwamish tribe of Washington State: *"Humankind has not woven the web of life. We are but one thread within it. Whatever we do to the web, we do to ourselves. All things are bound together. All things connect."*

I wondered what the odds were of finding a website that featured wolves and a quote that related directly to a poem I received not ten minutes earlier. In that poem, just like Chief Seattle, Wolf spoke of the strands in this giant web of which we are all a vital part.

Wanting to rule out the possibility of chance, I backed out of the website and returned to the browser. I clicked on the search box and changed my search parameters from *"meaning of dream catchers,"* to *"significance of dream catchers."*

Once again I clicked on the first URL in the list of results. The page that appeared displayed two eagles holding a banner that read, *"All are created equal in the eyes of God."*

The first paragraph attributed the origin of dream catchers to the Ojibwa Chippewa tribe. It explained how the Ojibwa tied strands of sinew around a bent wooden frame in the shape of a circle or tear drop. This much I had learned from the first site I had queried. I felt sure that I would find a similar description of dream catchers no matter how many different ways I worded my search. Still, I felt a need to continue reading. When I read the final line of the first paragraph, I stopped short, stunned anew:

"The patterns of the dream catcher," the site explained, *"would be similar to how these Native Americans tied the webbing for their snowshoes."*

102

If those in the spirit world wanted to convince me that there are no coincidences, they picked an excellent way of doing it. Twenty-four hours earlier Sanaya had made my finger twitch to announce that they had something to share. The first word they gave me was "snowshoes." I initially balked, hesitant to believe I was hearing the word correctly. When they insisted that I trust them, I faced a choice. I could decide that I had simply imagined the word and ask for another message, or I could do as they said and write it down.

Happily, I chose to listen. I had learned from experience that when I trust my unseen helpers, life unfolds in magical ways. The message that followed advised us to *see the world as it really is, not as our physical senses report it to be.* There are some things that happen in this world that cannot be explained without an understanding of a greater reality.

I no longer felt the need to look at other websites and learn more about dream catchers. I understood Wolf's message loud and clear: He included a dream catcher in his final drawing to show how interconnected all things are.

In the past few months I had become entangled in a web with a young man who died the same way my step-daughter had died. Wolf knew when he drew his dream catcher that each of us is one strand in a giant web of consciousness. Through him I was learning that the weave of that web is finer than most of us realize. We discover this for ourselves when we open our eyes and notice the signs that are all around us, whether they be as glaring as a billboard on a bus or as subtle as a still small voice that speaks of snowshoes in August.

CHAPTER THIRTEEN

On A Mission

At least once a year Ty's lower back goes into spasms. Every time it does, he blames it on his age, and every time I remind him that it stems from a bad muscle strain he had suffered in his early thirties. These same spasms erupted again the morning I received the poem from Wolf about the web. Ty had come back from walking the dogs, and when he bent over to unclip Rudy's leash, cried out in pain. I jumped to his side as his hands went to his back. But it was too late. The damage was done.

With bed rest the only remedy, he encouraged me to get out and enjoy Lake Louise on my own. While I didn't want to leave him, I recognized an opportunity to carry out Velvet's special mission. After making sure that Ty was comfortable, I gathered what I needed for the outing.

Velvet had given me a four-inch piece of clear quartz that she specially selected for its amplifying ability. I now placed that crystal in a small backpack along with my iPhone, a pair of headphones, my camera, wallet, and a bottle of water. I kissed Ty, petted Rudy and Gretchen, and headed out in the Honda to fulfil my sacred solo mission.

As I drove past the entrance to the campground, I noticed a spider's web glistening on the corner of the park ranger's guard shack. I flashed back to Wolf's drawing of a dream catcher and the synchronicities I had experienced with the two websites just an hour earlier. Suddenly, I had to have a dream catcher of my own.

This posed a challenge. We were camped in the national park just outside the tiny hamlet of Lake Louise. Tourists looking for shopping, fine dining, and nightlife stay in Banff, not in remote Lake Louise. The lake itself is located three miles up a steep, winding road from what euphemistically is referred to as "The Village." The sole amenities available to tourists there are clustered around

Samson Mall, a misnomer for two long buildings housing a grocery and liquor store, a bookstore, sporting goods store, a bakery, and one small gift shop. The likelihood of finding something as exotic as a dream catcher in such a collection of rudimentary retail establishments seemed remote, at best. Nonetheless, I decided to stop by the mall on my way to the lake and try my luck.

When I walked into the gift shop a few minutes later, the young First Nations woman working behind the counter must have wondered why I stopped in the doorway and laughed out loud. I'm sure she had no idea what I found so funny about a display rack filled with dream catchers. She returned my broad smile, however, when I purchased a beautiful creation with light brown feathers and a small quartz crystal in the center of the webbing. With her help, I added two pairs of earrings to my purchase: a set of dangly dream catchers set in sterling and a small pair of mother of pearl wolves.

I returned to the car with packages in hand and with lighter footsteps. Before starting the drive up the mountain I removed the wolf earrings from their small box and put them on. As I admired my new jewelry in the rearview mirror, I was filled with the sense that the wolves I saw reflected there would not be the only ones accompanying me on my upcoming hike.

I left the shopping center and joined a parade of cars heading to the parking area by the lake. The massive lots rivaled those found at major amusement parks with specially designed areas for tour buses. Even though it was not yet noon, cars were already parking on the grass along the roadside. I had hoped for some solitude, but after finding a spot for the car I found myself in a river of tourists meandering toward the lake.

My first view of Lake Louise revealed why up to fifteen thousand tourists visit its shores each day in the summer. The lake itself is only slightly longer than one mile in length, but the magnificent wilderness in which it sits is the source of its attraction. At the far end of the lake, two mountains slope down to its shores from either side to form a perfect "V" that is so pleasing to the eye. Beyond them, glaciers grace the summits of distant peaks, their runoff responsible for the lake's alluring emerald color.

The only ground suitable for building is at the eastern end of the lake. There, to my right, stood the grand Fairmont Chateau Hotel, offering its guests one of the most spectacular views in the world. To my left, tourists stood in line to rent red canoes from a picturesque boathouse. The weather could not have been more perfect for paddling or hiking. The sun shone brilliantly through puffy white clouds to cast a treasure trove of diamonds upon the lake's smooth surface.

Throngs of visitors lined the seawall for a quarter mile holding cameras and cell phones high to snap photos before returning to the parking lot. To my relief, I noted that beyond the paved section of the lakeside trail the crowd thinned out dramatically. The farther from the hotel, the fewer the people walking on the path.

I took a few photos of my own and began walking away from the hotel. After about a hundred yards, I came to a split in the trail where I stopped to read a sign indicating the names of the two trails that began at that point. Just like my life's work before and after our Susan's passing, they branched off in completely different directions. Ten years earlier I could not have imagined in my wildest dreams that I would one day embark on a mission to raise human consciousness by leaving a crystal in a lake. Doing such a thing was not a priority for the Joint Chiefs of Staff.

I recalled several of my tours of duty in the Navy during which I served as a protocol officer. My duties entailed planning elaborate ceremonies down to the smallest detail. Now I was about to conduct an important ceremony with Velvet's crystal and I realized I didn't have the slightest idea of where to go or what to do when I got there. In the past I would have been appalled at such a dismal display of planning. Now I enjoyed the peace and contentment that came from knowing that I would be expertly guided in my quest.

Before I could ask my unseen helpers for specific directions, a voice in my head said, *"Go to the end of the lake. There is a gift for you there."*

A flurry of excitement tickled my skin and I continued along the shoreline trail. I caught myself rushing and resolved to slow down to enjoy the journey as much as the destination. I normally savor the silence when outdoors, but I had brought music with me in case I wanted to spend time in one place and meditate. Now I decided to turn the hike into a walking meditation. I stepped to the side of the trail and pulled my iPhone and earbuds from my pack.

I plugged the headphones into the phone and flipped through my playlists in iTunes until I came to the Hemi-Sync music. I selected the *Portal to Eternity* CD and resumed my walk. The mystical Andean tones combined with the stunning scenery transported me quickly to an expanded state of consciousness. I was surprised, therefore, when a silent voice whispered, *"There is a better choice."*

I furrowed my brow and silently asked for clarification.

"There is a better choice in music," the voice said.

Curious, I raised the phone and peered at the screen. I had gone a bit overboard when I bought eight Hemi-Sync CD's at once, and had not yet listened to most of the collection. I had no idea what choice might be better than the tunes now playing in my ears until I scanned the list of titles. The answer soon stood out with unmistakable clarity and I found myself laughing again. Was it Wolf looking over my shoulder? I wasn't sure, but whoever it was knew that the better choice was a CD entitled *Dream Catcher.*

I selected the first song and set off toward the far end of the lake at an easy, measured pace. The ethereal music perfectly suited my mood as well as my surroundings as it transformed sight and sound into a symphony of the senses. Soft, haunting tunes seemed to highlight Nature's gifts such as the moss on the trees and the spongy pine needles under my feet. Shimmering high notes skipped across the surface of the lake on my left. The occasional ping of a drop of water sent my consciousness rippling outward until I blended completely with my environs in a visceral confirmation of the true meaning of oneness.

I came to a place near the end of the lake where the trail branched off to the right. Trees bordered most of the shoreline, but here a field of rocks formed a broad, open area along the water with a few boulders sized just right for a comfortable seat. Despite there being enough room for a dozen people to enjoy a bit of solitude, the few hikers near me on the trail continued on toward the higher elevations.

This is the spot, I thought.

I picked my way carefully across the rocks, allowing intuition to lead me until I found the perfect place to perform my ceremony.

I sat on a large, flat boulder and removed my backpack. With the fourth song from *Dream Catcher* playing in my ears, I reached inside the pack and pulled out Velvet's crystal. I laid the stone on my lap while I adjusted my posture and set my phone beside me. At that moment the name of the song I was listening to was *Lucid Dream.* Often I had experienced that magical state of being aware that I was dreaming. Whenever that happened, I would actively take part in the dream and see what fun I could create.

The title seemed fitting as I surveyed my dreamlike surroundings in the expanded state of consciousness that the music and walking meditation had engendered. Just as in my lucid dreams, I had actively created this unique moment, but as in most dreams, the outcome was uncertain. I didn't know if a crystalline grid actually existed around our Earth and if it had gaps that needed strengthening, but I was willing to do my part regardless.

I had certainly experienced the fluctuations in energy that exist from place to place around the planet and among its inhabitants. As I gazed out across the sparkling lake at the backdrop of majestic mountains, I was acutely aware of the refined energy in this sacred spot. It provided a natural "high" of the first order. I recalled Velvet's claim that Lake Louise was associated with the energy of Archangel Michael, and I nodded in understanding. If Michael indeed hovered around these hallowed waters, he could not have chosen a more fitting haven.

I lifted the crystal from my lap and held it in the palm of both hands. I thought of Wolf and the strands in the web that had brought me to this moment. Like Archangel Michael, Wolf's message spoke of love for all humanity and of freedom for the soul. If my actions that day could help to further their mission, I was honored to make the effort.

"Sitting in awareness of my oneness with All That Is," I prayed, *"I am so grateful for the gift of life. I affirm that my actions here today will help to raise the consciousness of all who inhabit this Earth. I see the placement of this crystal in this sacred setting blessing all of us and helping to strengthen the energetic grid that forms the pattern of our beautiful planet. I celebrate that all of us are coming to know ourselves as one with our Source and learning to love each other as souls on the same journey."*

With that, I transferred the crystal to my right hand and squeezed it tightly, imbuing it with the energy of my prayer. I then drew my arm back and threw the crystal in a high arc toward the center of the lake. As I watched the distant splash, two simple words came distinctly to mind.

Look up.

I lifted my gaze skyward and inhaled an involuntary breath. Tears of disbelief and wonder welled in my eyes and overflowed onto my cheeks. I had been told when I began my walk along the lake to go to the end, where I would receive a gift. That gift was now revealed in the sky above the mountain directly in front of me. Three towering cumulonimbus clouds merged together to form a head and shoulders at the center. Sweeping outward from behind the shoulders were two unmistakable angel wings.

I quickly pulled the camera from my backpack and snapped several pictures as the wings dissolved before my eyes. Within seconds, the clouds were gone, but the gift remained, preserved forever in my camera and in my heart.

I felt lightheaded, stunned by what I knew was confirmation that my efforts were noticed and appreciated. I sent Velvet a silent *thank you* for allowing me to be her surrogate and to experience this magical moment. With perfect timing to mark the conclusion of my ceremony, the *Dream Catcher* CD came to an end. I glanced down at my iPhone and for the third time that morning laughed out loud. The title of the final song now displayed on the screen was *Balance Restored*. I dried my tears and acknowledged yet one more wink from Wolf that indicated all was in perfect order.

I looked around for someone who could take a picture of me to memorialize this special day. Since my arrival at the rocky beach, the lone woman who had joined me now sat thirty yards away on a rock at the water's edge. She was of Asian descent with a round face framed by long, straight dark hair. She wore khaki slacks, a plain khaki T-Shirt, and no make-up. I guessed her age to be in the neighborhood of 55.

As I made my way carefully towards her, I noticed that she appeared to be enjoying a sacred moment of her own. I paused, hesitant to disturb her privacy. When she looked up at me and smiled, I returned the smile and stepped closer.

"I'm sorry to interrupt you," I said, "but would you mind taking my picture?"

"Not at all," she replied and took the camera I held out towards her.

"I just had a special experience on that rock over there," I said, pointing behind me, "So if you'd take several pictures of me from here that would be perfect."

I showed her how to use the Nikon's auto focus and returned to where I had left my backpack. Instead of facing the camera and posing with a smile, I stared out at the water and then up at the sky as she held the camera to her eye. While she was taking the photos, a tiny chipmunk wandered over to investigate me. I held out my hand and laughed with joy as the little creature sniffed my fingers and then scampered across my lap.

Thrilled that I had switched to the telephoto lens that morning, I shouted across to the woman, "Did you get that?"

"I think so!" she called back.

I retraced my steps to the shoreline. "Thank you so much," I said as I reached for the camera.

As she handed it back to me, our eyes locked and I instantly became aware of a shift in my state of consciousness. Time seemed to stop. We held each other's gaze, and what I saw inside her dark, almond-shaped eyes was pure love looking back at me. The feeling stunned me, and I wondered if she felt it too.

Until that moment, I had no intention of telling her why I had come to the lake. Now, with my heart opened wide, I felt drawn to share the awe of what I had just experienced.

"I'm here today for a special reason," I said. "I have come to leave a crystal in the lake. It's supposed to help strengthen the energetic grid around the Earth."

She stared back at me and I smiled awkwardly, suddenly aware of how silly my words must have seemed to her. And then, without saying a word, she reached into the backpack by her side and pulled out a four-inch quartz crystal. She held it up to make sure I saw it, and then laid the crystal reverently on a rock between us. My eyes widened in surprise as she then dipped back into her pack and retrieved another crystal, followed by another, and another until there were seven clear crystals lying side by side on the rock.

With her treasures now spread before her, she finally broke the silence and confirmed that she had come for the same reason I had. The only difference between our missions was that instead of being sent by an acquaintance, she claimed to have received direct guidance from the spirit world, just as Velvet had.

Keen to document this amazing coincidence, I asked if I could take her picture, and she allowed me to snap several poses. I made sure to include the crystals in the shots. I then introduced myself, and she told me her name was Elaine. I reached into the pocket of my shorts and handed her one of my cards, which identified me as an author and speaker.

"If you send me an email," I said, "I'll send you copies of the pictures."

The moment Elaine looked at my card, her energy completely changed. A blanket of darkness wrapped around her and she stared back at me now with unveiled wariness. She proceeded to share with me some experiences she claimed to have had that fell far outside my belief system. Her words suggested a state of paranoia that made the hair on my arms stand on end.

I flashed back to my days as the commanding officer of a transient personnel unit. Sailors being discharged for emotional instability were removed from their ships and sent to my barracks. As a result, I had become quite familiar with the signs of various personality disorders. Elaine was now displaying symptoms straight out of the *Diagnostic and Statistical Manual of Mental Disorders.*

She was clearly no longer pleased with my presence, and I suddenly longed to return to the blissful state I had enjoyed only moments earlier. I thanked her again for taking the pictures and made a hasty retreat to retrieve my belongings. As I began the hike back to my car, a thought popped into my head with such clarity that I almost stopped in my tracks: *Yes, she is imbalanced, but there is nothing wrong with her heart.*

I realized that Wolf had said nearly those same words during the reading I gave to his parents. I glanced back over my shoulder, ashamed that I had hurried away so quickly. I recalled the still-fresh memory of looking into Elaine's eyes and sharing a moment of pure spiritual love. My shame turned

111

to gratitude for the reminder that no matter how our challenges manifest in human form, the soul is the eternal expression of perfect love.

I slowed my pace and processed the morning's events as I finished the hike in silence. So many things that had happened since I awoke that morning in Lake Louise were synchronistic to the point of seeming surreal. I couldn't help but wonder if the whole experience wasn't some kind of cosmic lesson orchestrated from across the veil.

When I arrived back at the car I tossed all of my gear into the back seat except for my camera. I slid behind the wheel and turned on the camera in playback mode. Using the toggle switch, I slowly reviewed each photo on the small monitor. The pictures of the angel wings in the clouds left nothing to the imagination. I chewed on my lower lip, thrilled to have visual documentation of the magical morning. I had even snapped a screen shot of the *Dream Catcher* CD so I would remember to tell Ty about it.

Toggling forward, I saw with relief that Elaine had done an excellent job of taking my pictures. She captured perfectly the reverence I felt as I stared out at the lake after blessing the crystal. I flipped forward through a few more photos and laughed aloud when I saw the scenes with the chipmunk. Elaine caught a comical look of surprise on my face when he jumped onto my leg, followed by a spontaneous moment of arms-outstretched joy after he scampered across my lap.

The next series of photos were the ones I took of Elaine just after she had removed her crystals from her backpack. She smiled at the camera with a look of innocence that revealed nothing of the mental turmoil she manifested moments later. I might have been tempted to delete the photos had I not received a loving reminder from Wolf that allowed me to see beyond her human mask to the perfect soul inside.

I turned off the camera and laid it on the seat beside me. After starting the engine, I paused and glanced in the direction of the trailhead. I had gone to the lake in hopes of raising the consciousness of the planet. In the process, I learned a valuable personal lesson in seeing below the surface.

I put the car in gear and began driving down the mountain. I couldn't wait to get home to Ty with my heart filled to overflowing and my balance restored.

CHAPTER FOURTEEN

Perspective

The line of cars waiting to enter the United States at the border crossing in Couttes, Alberta stretched for more than a quarter mile. Ty was at the wheel of our new 42-foot coach when we pulled into the lane reserved for oversized vehicles. After inching forward for almost an hour, I offered to take over. Gratefully, he stood and rubbed his back, groaning from the stiffness as I slipped into the driver's seat.

With so little movement on the road, Ty was free to go back to the small kitchen and brew a pot of coffee. By the time he returned to the passenger seat with a steaming mug in hand, we had almost reached the inspection area.

"That looks a little tight," I said, pointing ahead.

In front of us, four lanes of traffic curved thirty degrees to the left before the final forty yards leading to the inspection booths. On both sides of each lane were rectangular metal scanners protected by five-foot high pilings painted a bright yellow. These pilings would not have been a concern were they not positioned just beyond the curve. The amount of space needed to turn our large coach was barely adequate to squeeze past without scraping it against those pilings. Towing the Honda behind us added to the challenge; our towing equipment did not allow us to back up.

"Do you want me to drive?" Ty asked.

"No, I've got it," I replied, harkening back to our days under sail when we often had to dock in narrow berths in the face of strong crosswinds. To keep our boating skills sharp, we always took turns at the helm whenever a tight spot loomed, regardless of weather or wind conditions.

Several vehicles were ahead of us as I began my final approach to the curve. My eyes darted back and forth from the left side to the right and the front, checking first the mirrors and then the actual view as I first applied my foot to the accelerator and then to the brake, allowing the nose of the coach to inch past the pilings. The process took so long that the roadway between us and the customs booth was now completely clear of cars that had already passed inspection.

"You need to pull up farther," Ty said.

"I can't tell how much room I have," I replied tensely.

Without another word, Ty opened the door and hopped down to the road. Walking to the front of the coach below the windshield, he beckoned me forward with both hands. I eased my foot off the brakes and moved ahead until he motioned me to the left. I shook my head, pointing at the right front corner of the coach which looked to be ready to scrape against a piling.

"Come on!" he said, still gesturing to my left.

Glancing ahead, I saw that the American customs officer had emerged from his booth and was observing our maneuvers with arms crossed and a none-too-pleased look on his face. To make matters worse, I was acutely aware that we were also being watched by everyone in our immediate vicinity and that we were holding up hundreds of cars in line behind us.

Ty had a better perspective than I, so I ignored my instincts and followed his directions. As he walked backwards, gesturing, I turned the wheel left, then right while inching forward with jerky motions that left the coach creaking. Rudy and Gretchen jumped into the passenger seat and looked about nervously, no doubt sensing my tension.

"It's okay, guys," I assured them. "We're almost there."

"You've got it!" Ty called out after a few more feet, and indeed I could now see in the mirrors that the back of the coach and the Honda would safely clear the pilings.

Ty opened the door and climbed back aboard. "Good job," he said as he set the puppies back in their beds on the floor between our seats.

"Thanks," I sighed with relief.

The inspection booth provided the final challenge, and I maneuvered slowly to get close to the window to converse without scraping our mirrors against the stall. The officer in charge continued to watch me negotiate the tight fit, taking a step backward into his doorway as I came alongside him and stopped.

I looked down at his dour face, his dark uniform, and the gun on his hip. "That was interesting," I said with the most ingratiating smile I could muster.

He held my gaze for a moment before turning away to study the full length of the coach. When he turned back to me, he nodded slowly and with a perfectly straight face said, "Now do it again."

I blinked in surprise, suddenly transported back to my Navy days when good-natured ragging was a way of life. I wiped the smile off my face, jutted out my chin, and glared back at him.

"No," I said with defiance.

He didn't smile, but a tiny flicker in his eyes gave him away.

We laughed in unison and I handed him our passports. He asked the standard questions about the purpose of our visit to Canada and didn't bother to inspect the coach. Within minutes we were headed south toward Great Falls, Montana, where we planned to spend the night at the campground on Malmstrom Air Force Base.

Our original schedule had us continuing east after leaving Montana and heading for Minnesota, where I had several events lined up in the Twin Cities in early September. We were looking forward to visiting friends in North Dakota and then making a side-trip to see Mount Rushmore for the first time. Unfortunately, our coach had developed several serious mechanical problems that demanded our attention. No RV repair facility along our planned route was able or willing to schedule the necessary warranty repair work. We therefore had to deviate a thousand miles and return to the dealer in Frederick, Colorado, where we had purchased the vehicle.

Ty and I had mixed feelings about this detour. We were understandably upset, of course, that our new RV already had major engineering issues. Unlike Ty, however, I looked forward to returning to Colorado. Three days earlier, when we had made the decision to head south rather than east, I had received a message from the spirit world.

There is a gift for you there, the voice said, exactly as it had on the trail at Lake Louise. I knew to trust that voice, and I felt a growing sense of excitement as we set out again for the Centennial State.

With Ty at the wheel of the coach, I opened the email app on my iPad. I noticed a new message from our friend, Terri Horsmann, whom we planned to visit in Minnesota once our coach was repaired. The subject line of her email read, "Ty's blog."

Terri was one of the most faithful followers of the quirky stories Ty shared online as we traveled around the country. He mentioned her frequently in his blog and referred to her as "Terri of the Frozen North." She and Ty often exchanged emails in which each tried to outdo the other with witty barbs. Upon seeing the subject line of the email waiting in my inbox, I wondered what aspect of Ty's latest blog had earned special mention. The opening line of her message made my eyes go wide in astonishment.

"Hey," Terri wrote, "you caught a wolf!"

I had no idea what she was talking about, but with all the Wolf-related synchronicities I had been experiencing during the past month, her choice of words stunned me. As it turned out, the wolf she was referring to had been in Ty's blog published two days earlier. In that blog he had described a scenic tour we had taken just before leaving Alberta along the Icefield Parkway, touted by National Geographic as one of the most beautiful drives on Earth. The photo he had chosen to insert in the write-up profiled the stunning view from Bow Summit in which jagged purple mountains towered over the turquoise waters of Peyto Lake far below.

"That lake is gorgeous," Terri wrote, "and it looks exactly like a wolf."

I opened a web browser and typed in the address for Ty's blog. As the page popped up on my screen, I stared at the photo to which Terri had referred and shook my head in confusion. I still had no idea what she was talking about. I went back to her email and smiled when I read her next line.

"If you can't see it," she wrote, "look at the top part of the lake. The two smaller coves are the ears, and the bigger cove to the right is the nose. It's the perfect wolf."

I returned to the blog and focused on the coves as Terri had suggested. Suddenly, the wolf jumped out from his hiding place and I beheld him in all his majesty. The change in perception was similar to what I had seen in drawings in which a dark vase set against a white background suddenly assumes the contours of a face depending upon which aspect of the picture the mind chooses to focus on. I was amazed that neither Ty nor I had seen the wolf in the photo. But he was there, waiting to be noticed.

Still shaking my head at Ty's choice of photographs out of dozens we had shot that day, I clicked on the next email. This one was from Libby, a friend in Florida who also was following Ty's blog. Just as Terri had, she asked if we had noticed how much the lake in Ty's photo looked like a wolf.

I replied to Terri and Libby, thanking them for bringing the wolf to my attention. Without delving into details, I told them that the wolf theme had been playing a prominent role in our summer's travels.

While I was responding to our friends, a new email appeared in my inbox. I recognized the address as that of Charles Cunis, a retired U.S. Army lieutenant colonel who had initially contacted me one year earlier after reading *Messages of Hope*. I have received many communications from readers touched by my book, but the email from Charles stood out because we shared a military background.

In his initial email he had described his battle with Parkinson's disease. Tired of taking pills to no avail, he had tried alternative therapies that included nutrition, integrative medicine, and CranioSacral Therapy. His search led him down a spiritual path laden with a new set of beliefs that caused his rigid, left-brained mind to rebel. At the height of his struggles he read an article about me and my work in a magazine published in his home state of Colorado. Intrigued to come across a spiritual teacher with a military background who had faced the same doubts he was currently battling, he decided to reach out to me.

"This old infantry officer never thought at age seventy that I would be experiencing this cornucopia of love, well-being, and gratitude for the gifts that I continue to receive," he wrote in that first email. "I never thought my zest for living would be so alive at this age. Your book and your meditation guide have helped me to put it all together and guide me in my pursuit of love, which is ultimately God. If you could spare the time and issue me a hip pocket summary on how you overcame your 'verify before you accept' training, I would be most grateful."

Instead of responding in writing, I picked up the phone and called the phone number he had included in his email. We enjoyed a delightful conversation during which he made me laugh repeatedly as he spoke in the colorful language typical of many Army officers I had known.

"Am I a whack job?" he asked after describing the formal Jesuit training that caused him to analyze every detail in his efforts to feel the love that was being manifested within him.

I assured him that not only was he quite sane, he and I were in fact kindred spirits. It was my need to verify new information, I told him, that had helped me to find greater faith. Further, I told him that while I thought it good to be skeptical, there is a big difference between being skeptical and being close-minded.

"The more we open our minds to possibilities," I said, "the more miracles happen."

"Yeah, well," Charles replied, "your message of love comes through *Lima Charlie* in your book."

I smiled at his use of radio code to describe a transmission that is *Loud and Clear*.

Now as I opened his latest email, I discovered that Ty's blog was once again the topic of discussion. For several weeks Ty had chronicled the frustrating problems we were having with the coach and our often fruitless efforts to deal with them. The entry immediately following our Icefield Parkway adventure announced that we had made the decision to return to the dealer in Frederick.

"I see that you're coming back to Colorado," Charles wrote. "I can imagine the demands on your time are quite extensive, but if there is any chance that we can get together, I would like to pick your brain some more. I am so grateful for your kindness to think about my Doubting Thomas conundrum. This kind of transformation just doesn't happen to 'crusty colonels.'"

Oh yes it does, I thought, as I clicked the "reply" button. It happens to Navy commanders and to anyone who is graced with the remembrance and knowledge of who we truly are.

I would have plenty of free time while the coach was being worked on, and I looked forward to meeting Charles. Near the RV dealer is a Starbuck's coffee shop, and I suggested to Charles that we meet there for coffee. Within a few hours of sending my suggestion he sent me another email to confirm a date and time.

Often the best laid plans do go astray, as ours did when Ty and I arrived at the dealership before the parts needed to make the necessary repairs to our coach. Faced with a delay of several days, we decided to do some hiking in Rocky Mountain National Park. I contacted Charles and we pushed our meeting back a week.

Ty and I enjoyed our stay at a campground in picturesque Estes Park. Each day, while we tried a different hike trail, I wondered if the gift promised to me in Colorado was this fortuitous opportunity to explore in such heavenly surroundings. Fortified by the exhilaration of being in the high mountains, we finally returned to the lowlands and set up camp in the dealer's parking lot. With the help of a strong cell phone signal there I was at least able to conduct readings as a medium and address the long list of people waiting to connect with their loved ones who had passed.

Repairs to the coach began on a Monday in late August. At nine-fifty that morning I walked into the Starbucks coffee shop where Charles and I had agreed to meet. None of the customers in view matched his description, so I bought a tall decaf and waited at a small table in the front corner. At one minute before ten o'clock a man who appeared to be in his early seventies pulled up in a light colored sedan and approached the coffee shop carrying a knapsack. He moved slowly but with purpose. I remembered Charles telling me that he was battling Parkinson's disease and felt certain that my friend had arrived.

I stood as he entered the door. He scanned the shop and when our eyes met, the broad smile that swept across his face confirmed that my hunch was correct. I held out my arms to him as he approached and said, "So, do crusty old colonels hug?"

"They sure do," he replied and returned the embrace.

We exchanged a few pleasantries, and then I waited while he went up to the counter to order a beverage. When he returned to the table and took a seat across from me, we chatted about the events that had brought us together. Charles refreshed my memory about his quest for alternative treatments for Parkinson's disease that had led him down an unexpected but most welcome spiritual path.

"You seem to be getting around pretty well," I said.

With that, he reached into the bag at his feet and produced a copy of Bruce Lipton's *The Biology of Belief.*

"Do you know this book?" he asked.

"Yes, I said. "I've read it. It's excellent."

He studied the cover before laying it on the table between us. "My CranioSacral therapist recommended this book to me," he explained. "After reading it, I became convinced that I could formulate a new approach to healing my symptoms by constantly sending positive stimulation to my cell structure. I was staggered by this knowledge."

"Most people do not understand the power of their thoughts," I observed.

Charles nodded. "Friends who had not seen me for some time were amazed at the progress I have made since putting Lipton's findings to good use. I'm by no means cured, but I've slowed down the disease."

He then reached back into his bag and pulled out a book I had not seen before: *The Tribe of Many Colors.*

"This is the second book my therapist recommended," he said. "The author is Kiesha Crowther, but she goes by the name of Little Grandmother. Her book provided me with my first exposure to Spirit. Her message is about Mother Earth and how we can interact with her. The message is beautiful and profound, but I was uncomfortable with it. The improved health I was experiencing with the CranioSacral therapy and this new spirituality were rubbing up against my military and Jesuit training. The kind of medical results I was experiencing should not have been happening."

I chuckled and said, "At least, not according to most people's belief systems."

"That's right," Charles agreed. "And then I found your book, *Messages of Hope*. I mustered up the courage to email you, and the rest is history. With Sanaya and your teachings, I've found my spiritual needs satisfied."

I shook my head, humbled by his words, and sent a silent thank you to my team of helpers in the spirit world for using me to help others.

Charles reached into his bag a third time and pulled out not just *Messages of Hope*, but several of my other books. "I was hoping you would sign these for me," he said.

"Do you have a kitchen sink in there, too?" I quipped, pleased but also a little embarrassed.

He shrugged. "I keep a stock of *Messages of Hope* and Lipton and Crowther's books to pass out as gifts when I feel they might help someone. So these two are for you."

He handed me his copies of *The Biology of Belief* and *The Tribe of Many Colors*, and I smiled at the unexpected gifts. It appeared that we shared a love of books.

I thanked him for his thoughtfulness and put the books in my purse. I then pulled out a copy of *Love Beyond Words*, my collection of daily messages from Sanaya. I held it near the copy he had just pulled from his bag and said, "I brought you a gift, too, but I see you already have it."

"I can't get enough of this stuff," Charles said enthusiastically. "I feel like a new person."

While I signed my books for him we discussed other titles that he might enjoy. Passionate about the same subjects, we chatted until I had to leave to get ready for a reading on the phone. We stood and hugged, and I thanked him again for the gifts.

I left the coffee shop and reached my car before Charles reached his. As I watched him from behind the wheel, I shook my head in wonder at his determination. For a man who should have been waylaid by a crippling disease, Charles Cunis was indeed a walking example of the power of belief.

That evening after dinner I settled onto the couch with a sense of deep satisfaction. I had enjoyed meeting Charles and experiencing the delightful energy with which he conducted his life. After I left him, I had had an equally rewarding reading over the phone. The connection with my client's loved one on the other side provided extraordinary evidence of his presence that left us both in awe.

I took a moment to give thanks. In spite of being locked in for the night in the RV dealer's asphalt lot, I had everything I needed: my loving husband, my two furry children, a comfortable home on wheels, a selection of my favorite music, and plenty of good books to read.

I glanced at the reading material stacked on the ottoman before me. Scraps of paper serving as bookmarks stuck out between the pages of three of the volumes. In the past, my linear brain would have required me to read every word in one book before moving on to another. Since I established a clear connection with the spirit world, however, I had learned to let Spirit guide my reading choice each day. The payoff came quite often when I would find either an exact reference to the message Sanaya had transmitted that morning or the answer to guidance I sought.

Now as I surveyed the stack of books, I felt drawn to the one on top of the pile. It was the second book that Charles had shown me that morning: *The Tribe of Many Colors* by Kiesha Crowther, distributed by Earth Mother Publishing. I picked it up and studied the cover, including a profile of a large tree sitting atop planet Earth beneath a sky filled with twinkling stars. A large spiral hovered to the left above the tree. With a start, I recalled that the spiral was one of the shapes Wolf had shown me during the reading with his parents.

I flipped to the back cover to see the summary statement of the book's contents. "The purpose of this book," it read, "is to re-ignite a deep remembrance within you of who you really are." I pursed my lips. My close connection with Sanaya and thousands of encounters with those in spirit during my readings had shown me quite clearly who we really are. I wondered why I felt guided to read this particular book when I already knew beyond a shadow of doubt that we are all spirit beings temporarily in physical form.

I opened the book to the introduction. The first paragraphs, written by Jennifer Ferraro, the book's editor, described Kiesha Crowther's mission to help heal Mother Earth. Unlike Charles, who had spoken earlier that day about the Divine Mother and Mother Earth, I had never spoken in terms of heavenly Fathers and earthly Mothers. Until I left the crystal in Lake Louise, my work focused primarily on helping to heal individual souls, not the planet as a whole. I again questioned why I now felt such a magnetic attraction to a book dealing with Mother Earth. Less than a minute later the answer to that question hit me like a blow to the head when I turned to the third page of the introduction.

"Like the other wisdom keepers," Jennifer wrote, "Kiesha would be responsible for certain crystals that were to be placed back in the Earth, to strengthen Mother Earth's ley lines and energy grid."

Startled by the synchronicity, I picked up a pen and drew an exclamation point in the margin alongside the words. Until one month earlier, I had never heard of efforts to place crystals around the planet. Now, just two weeks after I had left a crystal in Lake Louise, I was reading a book about it.

Inspired to see what other synchronicities I might find in the book, I read more quickly. I felt a kinship with Kiesha when two pages later Jennifer described how the thirty-year-old "Little Grandmother" often received specific guidance from Spirit, including information related to places unfamiliar to her. My heart started beating faster when I read that one of the places Kiesha was told about included an ancient site high in the Andes called Puma Punku.

The only other time I had read anything about the mysterious ruins in Bolivia was in *Twilight of the Gods,* the book I had seen move on the bookshelf in the Barnes and Noble store. In that book I found a photo of a statue with a name that I had never heard of, given to me by a young man in spirit.

I put an asterisk next to Puma Punku and wrote *"Pachamama"* at the bottom of the page. As I did so, I remembered that the ancients worshipped the statue as a fertility goddess. They also referred to her as the Earth mother, or Mother Earth, the subject of the book I now held in my hands and also the name of the book's distributor.

With mounting interest, I finished the introduction and turned to Part I, where a large spiral graced the opening page. I dived into the first chapter and learned that although much of Kiesha's work focuses on animals and Earth energies, we share a similar focus on love as the one Force that unites all living things. I felt as if Wolf were reading over my shoulder as I turned page after page, skimming past areas where I felt guided to move ahead.

I slowed when I came to a discussion highlighting the imbalance humans are experiencing between our masculine and feminine energies. I recalled the conversation with Velvet in Montana about the yin-yang symbol. Velvet told me that Wolf had come to work with me in helping to restore balance between these same energies.

Now as I read Little Grandmother's description about how the wisdom of Mother Earth can lead us back to a more balanced state, an image of the

Pachamama statue flashed in my mind. I suddenly realized that there was a greater purpose in the Pachamama discovery than simply to turn a "complete miss" from his unexpected visit into a "super hit." Still, if Wolf wanted to share a lesson about balance and Mother Earth, I couldn't understand why he had chosen a book about the Mayan Calendar to do so.

With a growing conviction that the book in my hands held the answer, I continued reading. Two pages further on I began a new chapter. When I read the opening sentence of that chapter, I froze. "There are two great civilizations that today hold the keys to living from the heart: The Mayans and the aboriginal people. They still live from the heart, and they are the ones who are teaching us now to live from the heart again."

Here in one crystal-clear paragraph was the missing piece from Wolf's initial visit. Wolf came to me in the dark and spoke of Pachamama, winged creatures, scientists conducting experiments, messages chiseled in stone, and an über-intelligent author. All these bits of evidence from across the veil had shown up in a book dealing with Mayan history, and now I knew why.

I re-read the opening sentences, this time focusing on words that stood out as if highlighted. *"Two great civilizations hold the keys to living from the heart: Mayans and aboriginal people."*

I recalled that Wolf's unexpected visit and the reading with his parents included references to Native Americans. Other than the dream catcher in his drawing, Mike and Beth could not explain the connection between Wolf and indigenous people. Now I realized that like the Mayans and the aboriginal people of whom Kiesha wrote, Native Americans still revered Mother Earth. Unlike the majority of humans today who stress logical thinking and strive for ever greater advances in science and technology, Native Americans follow heart-centered traditions that celebrate our interconnectedness.

Until now, Mike, Beth, and I had been puzzled by the information in Wolf's initial visit that made no sense compared to the extraordinarily high accuracy of the rest of the evidence he brought through that morning. Thanks to Little Grandmother's book, all of the pieces now held meaning.

I get it! I get it! I shouted silently to Wolf. He had been trying to tell me from the first time his spirit spoke to me that we as a people are out of balance.

"*Wow!*" I wrote in the book's margin. "*This is why Wolf led me to Pachamama. The 'gift' I was promised in Colorado is this book!*" I realized then that what had seemed like a casual get-together with Charles Cunis at Starbucks was a divinely guided date.

I wanted to call Mike and Beth to tell them about my discovery, but it was now close to ten o'clock. With great excitement I shared my discoveries with Ty and apologized that I would most likely be staying up later than usual. There was no way I could sleep until I had finished Little Grandmother's book.

With pen in hand I continued reading. I was familiar with most of the material in the succeeding pages. I had been teaching many of the same spiritual concepts for several years in my presentations about love-centered living. I was startled, however, when I came to a section in the book in which Kiesha described an image that was quite fresh in my mind, having recently shared it with Velvet in Montana.

"There were dots of light in various places all over the planet," Kiesha wrote. "The rest was blackness. These points of light are the souls living today whose hearts are in alignment, those who have raised their frequency and are living from the heart."

I drew a circle around that paragraph. This was the identical image and lesson that Sanaya had shared with me two years earlier on the day I received the download about the stellated dodecahedron. I marveled that Kiesha, Velvet, I, and most likely many others were now receiving and passing on the same message.

I dog-eared the page and pressed on. If I had any doubt that Wolf had meant for me to uncover his message hidden in this book, those doubts were dismissed when I reached the final chapter. With a sense of awe I read, *"The time of the lone wolf is over."* I circled the words along with the lesson that followed: "We are on the verge of a massive shift of consciousness that will change how we relate to each other and how we feel inside."

I starred the words *"A massive shift of consciousness."* This was what all of the fuss concerning 2012 was about. It was why my unseen helpers in the spirit world made Erich von Däniken's book about 2012 move so that I would be compelled to buy it.

The end of the Mayan calendar did not signal the end of the Earth. Instead, it heralded a new period in which our solar system is in alignment with the center of the Milky Way. Just as the moon affects our moods, we are affected by the movement of all celestial bodies. The alignment of our solar system with the *heart* of our galaxy opens a channel for higher cosmic energies to flow through all of us. The result is increased awareness of our interconnectedness with one another.

I flopped back against the couch and closed the book. As I stared at the spiral on the cover, I recognized the symbol as the perfect example of the metaphysical tenet, *"As above, so below."* Our galaxy is a massive spiral. As our Earth comes into alignment with our spiral-shaped universe, it is our task as spiritual beings to come into alignment with the center of our own individual universe: the heart.

I scribbled these concepts onto a notepad and thought of the wonder Mike and Beth would experience when I called them in the morning. I couldn't wait to tell them how hard their son had worked to help us humans see that the time had come to get out of the head and into the heart.

I closed my eyes and focused on Wolf's spirit to send him a heart-felt message. *Thank you for your persistence.*

I reflected on the past few weeks and the string of events that had kept Wolf in my awareness. I realized that he was not going to leave me alone until I finally understood his message. I thought of the dramatic way that he transitioned from this world, leaving behind a prophetic poem and a drawing that provide proof of a greater reality. There was a reason that he left the way he did.

In the reading with his parents, Wolf had said to his father. *"This is so others will pay attention. You're supposed to share this story."* I wasn't sure now if Wolf meant that Mike was supposed to share the story or if he had been referring to me. I certainly had a vehicle for doing so with my presentations and workshops, and Wolf's message fits perfectly with my mission of helping people to let their spirit soar.

I would speak to Mike and Beth in the morning and I would ask them if they would grant me the honor of sharing Wolf's lessons. I set the book and my notepad on the ottoman and turned out the light. Little Grandmother was right. The time of the lone wolf is over.

CHAPTER FIFTEEN

In The Flow

When I shared the platform with Dr. Eben Alexander at the *Soul Life* conference in Virginia Beach in May of 2013, I knew I would be seeing him again. Both of us were scheduled to speak five months later at an international conference on the island of Crete entitled, "Life, Death and Beyond." When Mike Pasakarnis approached me at that conference, I had no idea that he and Beth would later decide to travel halfway around the world to join us.

I called Mike and Beth the morning after I discovered the link between Wolf and the Mayans. When I asked if they would allow me to tell his story and share his message of living from the heart, they honored Wolf and me by saying yes. When they also told me that they had decided to splurge on the trip to Greece, I was thrilled. Thanks to Wolf, we had formed a special bond during the brief time we had known one another.

My mind kicked into high gear the moment I got off the phone. I checked my calendar and noted that the conference in Crete was less than six weeks away. I imagined the thrill of sharing my debut presentation about Wolf and his message with Mike and Beth in the audience. For a moment my human side tried to slip a few doubts into the jumble of thoughts racing through my mind. Six weeks was not much time to prepare, the voice nagged. I had enough to do without taking on a new project.

I pushed such thoughts aside, aware that I would never get anything done if I listened to the ego. I had faith that Wolf and Sanaya would show me the way and provide whatever wisdom and support was needed.

I have discovered in my life that when something is meant to happen, the Universe will conspire to help make it happen. In this instance the timing was truly divine. My next three speaking engagements were two weeks away in Minneapolis, and I was already well prepared for them. Our driving route from

Colorado would take us east across Kansas into Missouri and then north on I-35 through Iowa. Having nine hundred miles of corn, alfalfa, and wheat fields to drive through provided the perfect milieu for working on my "Wolf presentation" that I would be giving in Crete. There would be few distractions.

We departed the RV dealership on August 28th with a fully functional coach. Within an hour after leaving Frederic the traffic thinned down dramatically and shifted from foreign imports and luxury sedans speeding south on I-25 toward Denver to big lumbering trucks on I-170 carrying cattle and pigs.

As the Rocky Mountains receded in our rear view mirrors, I opened a new Power Point file and stared at the stark whiteness of the first blank slide. Up to this point I had not given a thought to a name for the presentation. The title needed to capture both Wolf and his message. Because I knew I had a co-author waiting in the wings, I directed my thoughts to Wolf and asked, *"What should I call this?"*

The answer came to me immediately. I clicked on the slide, inserted a text box, and typed in the words, *"Heart Gifts."*

Having opened the gate to Wolf's inspiration, ideas of how to piece together his story streamed into my conscious mind. Using photos provided by Mike and Beth and others I found on the Internet, I created a slide showing the A.R.E. headquarters and another with Mike in his wolf T-Shirt. I then placed a picture of the labyrinth in Virginia Beach next to Wolf's drawing done years earlier depicting the two yin-yang symbols with their matching dolphins.

I went on to piece together the days just before and after Wolf's passing. I sent a wave of gratitude to Mike and Beth for having the foresight to send a photographer through Wolf's apartment. I recognized the emotional impact that the chaotic floor-to-ceiling artwork would have on the many people who would now see inside Wolf's home and his mind. The photos of his poem and the tree with the roses were worth far more than a thousand words.

I paged through the slides to make sure they told the story exactly as it unfolded. Although I had reviewed the events in my mind countless times since Mike and Beth first shared them with me, the story never failed to amaze me. Here in the slides was visual proof that the soul has access to information that our conscious minds cannot perceive.

I turned to Ty, who had been driving across the Great Plains in silence while I did my work. "People are not going to believe this story," I said, even though I knew in my heart that they would.

Ty confirmed my thoughts when he replied, "Yes, they will, because the evidence is so credible."

I continued working on the presentation throughout the day, taking breaks here and there to relieve Ty at the wheel. He willingly endured longer shifts than normal, knowing that I had set a short deadline for myself. Still, I felt sorry for him. The drudgery of driving past scenery that changed little hour after hour stood in stark contrast to the excitement and wonder of what I was doing.

"People who live out here certainly are independent," I commented at one point when I came up for air and gazed out at the legendary spacious skies and amber waves of grain stretching from horizon to horizon.

"Yeah, well, you missed the sign a few miles back," Ty commented dryly. "Quinter, Kansas, population 918. Free land and water. Move here." I smiled as he added, "What does that tell you?"

"It tells me that some folks truly love living out here, and they want others to love it too. It's sort of like being at sea, isn't it?"

"Point taken."

We stopped to stretch our legs at a rest area, groaning as we stepped outside into temperatures that exceeded a hundred degrees. Even Rudy and Gretchen seemed in a hurry to get their business done and get back on the road.

Underway again, I returned to my task. I opened the folder containing my notes from Wolf's unexpected visit and the typed transcript of his reading. From these pages I chose a sampling of the unique details that allowed Mike and Beth to fully comprehend that the information I received had come straight from their son. I made a slide with a list of the evidence provided that included the symbols he drew, the sacred ceremonies, the writings and drawings, and various character traits that matched Wolf perfectly.

When I reread the sections in the reading in which Wolf brought up his poor grades, his inability to hold down a job, and the word "schizophrenia," I again shook my head in wonder. I had yet to experience anything less than an outpouring of love and intelligence from Wolf's pure spirit. This loving essence that is present in all souls was a key message I wanted to convey to my audience.

Ty's voice interrupted my thoughts as he announced, "We're coming up on Victoria."

I lifted my gaze from my computer to the scenery unfolding ahead. In the distance I could see the tall twin spires of St. Fidelis Church rising like an oasis amid the corn fields. Known as the "Cathedral on the Plains," it was listed as one of the eight wonders of Kansas. As such, it was Victoria's claim to fame.

"Oh, it's so cool to be here!" I said, clapping my hands like a little child.

It wasn't the church that had me so excited. It was the town. Victoria was the boyhood home of Wayne Knoll, the priest I featured in my book, *The Priest and the Medium*. In 2008 when I began interviewing medium Anne Gehman to write her biography, I realized that the story needed a "hook" to make it stand out. That hook, I realized, was Anne's husband, Dr. Wayne Knoll, Ph.D., a former Jesuit Priest and professor of literature at Georgetown University. I often joked that a story about a medium married to a former Catholic priest gave my book "mass" appeal, and indeed, readers were drawn to this loving couple's unique story.

In the process of interviewing Wayne about his fascinating life, he shared numerous fond memories of his formative years in tiny Victoria, Kansas. Many of these included stories of his days as an altar boy at St. Fidelis Church. Wayne and I discussed his home town in such detail that I felt as if I had personally walked its streets, even though I did not visit it until three years after the book was published.

Now as we approached the exit for Victoria, Ty asked if I wanted to stop there again.

"No thanks," I said with a chuckle. Been there, done that." We had enjoyed a short visit on our way west through Kansas two years earlier. The few residents with whom we chatted were certainly friendly, but other than revisiting the church, there wasn't much reason to stop.

I had thought of Wayne and Anne several times during the past few months, but every time I had tried to reach them my call went to voicemail. With the town of Victoria now passing by on my right, a little voice told me to try again. I picked up my cell phone, found Anne and Wayne's home number, and placed the call. To my delight, Anne picked up on the second ring.

"Anne!" I said with excitement. "It's Suzanne, and at this moment I am looking out the window of our coach at Victoria, Kansas!"

"Oh, my," she said in the soft, lilting voice that always brought a smile to my face. That smile quickly faded, however, when Anne told me that Wayne was seriously ill. The reason they had not been answering calls was because doctors had found an inoperable tumor wrapped around Wayne's aorta.

"He's been in a lot of pain," Anne said, "but I think it would do him a world of good to hear your voice. Would you like to talk with him?"

"Absolutely!"

When Wayne came on the line, I would not have known anything was wrong with him. Rather than focus on his illness, we talked about Victoria and laughed about the differences between his home town in Kansas and his life now in the nation's capital. I smiled and felt my heart expanding in response to Wayne's loving vibration.

I didn't want to tire him by talking too long. Nonetheless, I hated to end the conversation because I had the strong sense these would be our last words to each other in this lifetime. I told him that I loved him, and after we said goodbye, I leaned my head back against the seat and closed my eyes, transported back in time to the moment years earlier when Wayne Knoll made a statement that changed my life.

"A truly spiritual person loves everyone," he announced one day when I was interviewing him for my book. His words struck a blow against my chest. At that early stage in my own spiritual journey, I had admitted to myself that I did not feel love for all others, and I didn't like that sensation. I have always believed, however, that if anyone on this planet has done something that I wish to do, there is no reason I can't do it, too. *Sandy!*

I longed to love other people the way Wayne Knoll did, and I made it my goal at that moment to be more like Wayne. In a special prayer, I asked God to show me how to look upon all others with love. The answers I received have become teaching points that I now share in my workshops, but I did not receive this state of grace without some emotional housecleaning. Thanks to my role model, Wayne Knoll, I learned through personal experience how it feels to love all of my fellow human beings by seeing past our differences to the purest essence of each individual. It is that essence that connects us all to each other and to God.

Three months after our phone call, Wayne passed to the other side at age eighty. He left behind a legacy of love that spread like ripples through the countless lives he had touched. He personified the concept of oneness, which is what Wolf was guiding me to share in the *Heart Gifts* presentation.

I continued matching slides with ideas as we traveled north from Kansas City through Missouri. Teaching points flooded my mind as I worked with the topic of balance and the yin-yang symbol. I was shown very clearly by Wolf and Sanaya how to express the thoughts visually, many of them utilizing the shapes Wolf showed me in his two initial visits.

I had never enjoyed the study of geometry when I was a high school student, but now as a teacher of personal transformation I am fascinated by the field of sacred geometry. This branch of metaphysics provides a way to understand creation and the evolution of the soul using the symbolic values of shapes. Each shape provides a framework for our experiences, and my guides were now urging me to teach the importance of the stellated dodecahedron around our planet along with a shape that I was reading about more often in my studies: the torus.

I found no shortage of these figures on the Internet, but I wanted to make slides that matched the geometric shapes with the ideas Wolf was showing me. Unfortunately, I lacked the skills to create professional graphics with that level of detail. As I sorted through the list of my friends who possess both creative ability and computer savvy, one man stood out head and shoulders above the others: artist Barry Mack.

I had remained in touch with Barry while making arrangements to ship his "Going Home" painting from Oregon to Florida. On several occasions I had received further insights for him from Sanaya that he confirmed were spot on. I felt awkward asking an artist whose work hung in fine galleries and elegant homes to provide pro bono assistance for a slide show, but I knew that Barry would understand the importance of my request. Indeed, he responded to it with great enthusiasm. Within days he sent me a selection of beautifully crafted digital drawings that perfectly matched the images I had in mind to reinforce the key points in my upcoming slide shows.

As Wolf's message continued to take shape, Ty and I traveled on into Iowa. Driving through the heartland of America proved to be the perfect time to put together a talk about living from the heart. When we pulled into the small farming community of Perry for the night, we were treated to a taste of true Midwestern hospitality.

Ty had called ahead and made arrangements to park at the Elk's lodge in Perry. We often stayed in their parking lots when traveling through areas with no campgrounds. The lodge member Ty spoke with apologized for having only a fifteen amp outlet for us to plug into for electrical power. We were therefore stunned when we arrived at the lodge to discover that a member had wired a fifty amp outlet just for our overnight stay. This unexpected act of kindness allowed us to run the coach's air conditioners in the ninety degree late summer heat.

The cool air allowed me to comfortably enjoy an extended session in meditation early the next morning before breakfast. I had not intended to sit longer than my usual twenty to thirty minutes, but just as I was coming out of the deeper trance-like state, I saw the wolf's face. What followed were a series of images and instructions showing me a new way to bring my body, mind, and spirit into alignment.

Until that morning, whenever I meditated I visualized myself sitting in a shaft of bright, white light, opening myself to the downward flow of higher cosmic energy. Without this Life Force flowing through us, we would not breathe. By focusing on this flow, we are brought into conscious communion with the higher realms of the spirit world.

What I did not realize until that morning in Perry, Iowa was that my visualization of the energy flowing in from above was only half of the picture. From the moment we take in our first breath at birth until we exhale for the final time at death, we are living in both spirit and human form. Our physical bodies are made of the same earthly substance as the ground around us. From dust our bodies have come and to dust they will return as our soul continues its eternal journey. In the meantime, we nourish our physical bodies with food and with the unseen energy and support from Mother Earth.

By visualizing the flow of energy only from above, I was subtly and inevitably out of balance. Wolf and Sanaya showed me that this was why I often found myself physically drained after giving a reading. While I had been consciously replenishing the spirit, I had failed to recharge the body with the same mindful intent. Now they showed me the energy flows from high above as well as from the core of the Earth below. In this clear vision I saw these two distinct streams of energy meeting at the heart, the bridge between the two worlds and between us all, as both spiritual and physical beings.

I applied their teaching by doing exactly as they showed me. I moved my consciousness down the shaft of light to the very center of the Earth. Breathing in, I drew a strong current of Earth-energy up the shaft of light directly to my heart. I did this a second time and then moved my conscious thought as high up the shaft as I could imagine. I inhaled and imagined a clear stream of spirit-energy flowing down from there directly into my heart.

I repeated the downward breath a second time and then imagined the energy continuing to flow on its own from above as well as from below. Suddenly I became lightheaded, a signal I had learned from giving my readings that I was shifting to a higher state of consciousness. Curious, I surrendered to the experience, and when I did, the "I" who had been sitting in a chair in a coach in the parking lot of an Elks lodge in Perry, Iowa disappeared.

My awareness of my physical body vanished, and I became a particle of light. I was infinitesimally small, a mere speck of consciousness within the light in which I had been sitting moments earlier. At that instant I existed both everywhere and nowhere. It was a sensation of simultaneous expansiveness and nothingness such as I had never before experienced, and I heard the words, "This is balance. This is alignment."

Later, after checking the clock, I realized that I had meditated for only a few minutes longer than usual that morning; but in that expanded state, time had lost all meaning and relevance. I had experienced first-hand the heart-centered oneness that Wolf wished me to speak about, and it was pure bliss. When I returned to full waking awareness, it was not without a tinge of regret.

I understood then why we all yearn to go home, whether or not we are conscious of that yearning. We long to return to our natural state of wholeness. This longing and "homesickness" is akin to the feeling humans experience after the loss of a beloved partner. We so fully identify with our loved one that we feel as if part of our own self has died and gone missing. This feeling, as I experienced in the meditation, is an illusion. We are not separate physical beings. We are pure spirit interconnected by a light that can be neither divided nor dimmed. It is only when we embrace all sides of our true self—the physical as well as the spiritual—that we experience wholeness and the joy of pure "being."

Most humans are unaware that we are spirit beings temporarily existing in human form. Their consciousness is therefore focused on the human drama with all of its ups and downs and ins and outs. Conversely, some individuals following a spiritual path eschew their human nature once they understand and embrace their higher selves. Neither approach leads to peace. Like the yin and the yang in the symbol Wolf drew so often, our physical bodies and our spirit bodies dance in harmony, making up two sides of a whole. When we focus on one side of our wholeness and ignore the other side, we are out of balance.

If I felt disappointment at finding myself once again in a human body, that feeling disappeared when I recognized the gift that Wolf and Sanaya had given me. They had shown me a method of achieving the state of unity through a simple breathing technique that brought mind, body, and spirit into proper alignment. I knew it was a technique they wanted me to share with others.

Having experienced bliss, the desire to float away remained strong within me. The physical body, however, has a way of bringing one quickly back to Earth. My stomach grumbled, reminding me that I hadn't yet eaten. The loud bang of a compartment door in the belly of the coach told me that Ty was preparing to break camp and get on the road. I stamped my feet to get grounded and stepped back fully into my role as a human being.

Five hours later the corn fields of Iowa seemed light years away when we found ourselves navigating within the web of lakes and highways surrounding Minnesota's Twin Cities. My speaking engagements in Minneapolis were not until later in the week, so we continued northwest to the aptly named Chain of Lakes campground. We chose the location based upon its proximity to Coon Rapids, home of our friend *Terri of the Frozen North*. We not only ribbed Terri unmercifully about her state's frigid weather, but also about the name of her town. She had promised to show us that Coon Rapids was far more cosmopolitan than its name suggested.

With our coach's high-tech systems, setting up camp was a breeze. When Ty pointed out that it was after five o'clock and offered to pour two glasses of wine, I asked him if he minded waiting thirty minutes. All day I had been deluged with ideas of how to cogently work the techniques shown to me that morning into a guided meditation for the *Heart Gifts* presentation. Before enjoying "happy hour," I wanted to record the steps that had given me such a profound experience.

Ever supportive, Ty went for a walk with the dogs to check out the campground. I gathered my tape recorder and my favorite meditation music and sat on the couch. Because Mike and Beth would be among the first to hear the guided meditation, I imagined that they were in the room with me and I asked Wolf to join us. I took a few cleansing breaths and then turned on the music and started the recorder.

I shifted my focus to the higher realms and began speaking aloud as if guiding Mike and Beth through the introductory breathing process of the meditation. I walked them through the steps to join the earthly and spirit energies at the heart. When I reached the point of visualizing the body dissolving, the music playing in the background struck a magical note that transported me to a higher state. There I was inspired to recite the lines of Wolf's final poem. The words of that poem fit perfectly with the purpose of the session as I prayed aloud to the spirit of the Great Healer to awaken within the heart.

After finishing the session, I decided to send the recording to Mike and Beth. I was curious to see if the process would affect them as deeply as it had affected me. I uploaded the audio file onto my computer and opened a blank email. When I noticed the date, September 8th, I realized the significance of the time of this gift. It was three years to the day since Wolf's spirit had crossed to the other side.

I attached the recording to the email and wrote a short message. "Know that on days like today, Wolf is more present with you than ever."

The next morning I received a reply from Mike. "Thank you for the heart meditation," he wrote.

"When we heard you recite Wolf's words it caught us both by surprise, but then they seemed to fit in and flow so naturally that it only added to the overwhelming experience. I can't wait to keep practicing this. I've tried to meditate many times, but this technique brings me to a different realm, and I hope to be able to more fully experience the feeling of just Consciousness. I have difficulty choosing words sometimes because of the immense spirituality of these experiences, but I hope you can understand what I'm trying to say."

I understood exactly. Even for a writer, it is challenging to describe experiences that take place in a dimension where communication occurs without words.

Mike ended his email by writing, "We are both so grateful to you for all of these gifts and for your thoughts, support and kind words on this angelversary day."

I smiled at his choice of words. "Angelversary" was a fitting term for the date Wolf passed, for surely he now dwells among the angels. Having repeatedly felt his powerful energy, I have no doubt that is true. I also had no doubt after reading Mike and Beth's reaction to the meditation technique that Wolf wanted me to include it in the *Heart Gifts* presentation.

I felt a shiver of excitement as I envisioned sharing Wolf's story and the meditation with other people. Thanks to the near constant inspiration from Wolf and Sanaya on our journey across the Great Plains, I had been able to put his message into a presentable form far faster than I had imagined. The conference in Crete where I hoped to debut the talk was still a month away.

Suddenly I didn't want to wait even that long.

CHAPTER SIXTEEN

Heart Gifts

From outside, the Center for Spiritual Living of St. Louis, where I was scheduled to speak, looks like a private home. It sits on a large grassy plot of land across from the public library and the Parkway North High School. The parking lot behind the church is barely large enough for us to park the coach.

While Ty pulled the power cord from the utility compartment, I walked to the front of the church and entered the security code in the cypher lock on the front door. When the door clicked open I sent a silent thank you to Reverend Marigene and her staff for trusting us to make ourselves at home in their church.

I stepped into the foyer and paused a moment to inhale a cleansing breath. Sacred places have a special feel about them, and I gratefully soaked up the peaceful energy after a long day on the road. I took a few steps and stopped in the doorway to the sanctuary. The dim lighting added to the feeling of serenity that enveloped me. I hoped to fill the seats during the next two evenings, but for now I was content to revel in the quiet sanctity of my surroundings.

It was only four months earlier that I had addressed this same congregation. My sermon and events were so well received that the senior minister, Reverend Marigene De Rusha, invited me to speak again in September on my way home. We had agreed that the subject of my talk on the return trip would focus on how to attune to higher consciousness. Because Marigene had been out of the country during our first visit, Ty and I looked forward to meeting her and to once again enjoy the unrivaled enthusiasm and love of her congregation.

When I saw that Ty had planned an extra day in St. Louis after my *Making the Connection* event, I realized that I could add a dry run of *Heart*

Gifts on the second night. I drafted a short email to Marigene summarizing the new presentation and proposing the addition to the schedule. Sanaya had taught me, *"When your heart's in the right place, things fall into place,"* and true to their word, the day after Wolf's angelversary, Reverend Marigene wrote back to express her great enthusiasm. "Let's do it!" she said.

Now as I stood inside the church, I gave thanks for the opportunity to tell Wolf's incredible story. Suddenly, several loud knocks on a door shattered the silence and I winced. I left the sanctuary and hurried through the fellowship hall to the back entryway. There stood Ty on the other side of the glass panes holding our orange extension cord.

"Sorry," I said as I pushed the door open.

"Did you get lost?" he asked good-naturedly.

"Sort of," I answered.

He stepped inside and plugged the cord into an outlet. As we returned to the coach together, a sedan pulled into the lot. Recognizing the driver, I smiled. Dave was one of the church members who had shown us remarkable hospitality when we passed through in May.

We greeted each other with a hug.

"Welcome back!" he said, before shifting his gaze to our coach. "Didn't you have a different bus four months ago?"

I gave Dave a sheepish smile. Without looking at my husband I said, "Yes, we did. This one was a bit of a spontaneous purchase."

Ty cleared his throat.

As Dave nodded approvingly, his gaze still fixed on the coach, I changed the subject before Ty could make a joke about women shoppers.

We chatted for a few more minutes before Dave excused himself and went inside the church. I looked around at the familiar surroundings now with a sense of déjà vu mixed with inevitability. Just as we hadn't planned on buying a new RV when we left Florida, neither had we planned on returning to St. Louis and giving two back-to-back presentations. When I agreed to speak to the congregation again, I had no idea that the spirit of a young man named Wolf would come into my life and give me a story so powerful that I would feel compelled to share it.

I thought about the poem Wolf had written in which he spoke of peace and tranquility flowing like water. The ability to flow with unexpected changes had brought us to this place. I felt no trepidation, only excitement and trust that Wolf and my other helpers in the spirit world would not let me down when I unveiled my *Heart Gifts* presentation.

I mustered that same trust later when Reverend Marigene knocked on the door of the coach. She had asked if I could give her a reading while we were in town, and I happily agreed to do so. I was going to speak that evening about "making the connection" and I wanted her to know why I could state with authority that all of us have the ability to tap into higher consciousness.

Although we had never met face-to-face, we greeted each other like old friends. I instantly felt that my initial impressions of Marigene were correct. I had learned in the Navy how the leader of a unit or an organization can affect its morale and efficiency. When Ty and I met the enthusiastic and caring members of CSL St. Louis, we both knew that much of the credit for the high energy in the church went to ministers Marigene and Larry De Rusha.

Marigene's loving nature no doubt contributed to the excellent connection I experienced with the spirit world during her reading. She enjoyed a virtual family reunion as six of her relatives and one friend who had passed to the other side provided verifiable evidence of their presence that left both of us in awe.

The reading was my gift to Marigene. She returned the gift that evening when she introduced me to a full house in the sanctuary and shared the details of her reading with those gathered. Her praise of the evidence set the stage for me to speak with confidence about the continuity of consciousness and the existence of the unseen dimension.

I stepped onto the platform to a chorus of cheers and whistles befitting a rock star. I shook my head in amazement. Normally I would wonder if the crowd had been engaged in some pre-game drinking, but they had reacted the same way when I delivered my sermon four months earlier on a Sunday morning. This group was perpetually happy, drunk on love.

At the end of my three-hour *Making the Connection* presentation, I invited all present to join me again the next evening. "If the information and the evidence you heard tonight helped to expand your view of reality," I said, "the story I'm going to share with you tomorrow night will take your beliefs to a whole new level. I'm going to introduce you to a young man in spirit who will leave no doubt in your mind that this world is not all there is. The message he has come back to share is one you won't want to miss."

I lay in bed that night wondering if I had built a strong enough case to coax people from their homes two nights in a row. I need not have worried. Ty and I greeted a steady stream of guests in the lobby of the church the next evening as the sanctuary filled to the brim a second time. Ten minutes before seven o'clock I excused myself and retreated to an empty classroom. I took a seat in one of the hard-backed chairs, closed my eyes, and took several deep breaths.

"Oh God, Wolf, and my team of helpers on the other side," I prayed, *"thank you for this opportunity to bear your message this evening. I ask that you guide my thoughts and words so that those gathered receive the highest possible wisdom. May the consciousness of the whole be raised by these teachings, and may all of us experience the joy and preciousness of your presence."*

Upon finishing the prayer, I felt my torso twitch involuntarily. I was well familiar with this sign from Sanaya, and I thanked my team for their physical confirmation that I would not be stepping onto the platform alone.

I returned to Ty's side in the lobby and squeezed his hand.

"Ready?" he asked.

"You bet," I replied.

At seven o'clock, with no need for a second introduction from Reverend Marigene, I stepped onto the platform. The crowd was equally enthusiastic as the night before, and I waited until they settled down before welcoming them back to the church.

"As most of you know," I began, "Ty and I have been enjoying a journey around the country since we were here in May. Tonight I'm going to share a remarkable story that unfolded quite unexpectedly on that journey. Some of you may find the details hard to believe, but I can assure you that every one of them is true. I will show you photographs and provide evidence that prove we are part of a much greater reality than the one we perceive with our physical senses.

"All of us walk in two worlds at once:" I stated, "the world of matter and the spirit world. Tonight I'm going to reveal how deeply interconnected these two worlds are. I'm going to unravel a web of clues left to me by a very special soul on the other side. At the center of that web is a lesson that we humans need to hear now more than ever."

I brought the opening slide onto the screen. "I have entitled this presentation '*Heart Gifts*' and I am going to take you on a journey to the center of your individual universe: the heart. Come with me now to the place this story began, at a conference in Virginia Beach, Virginia."

With that, the audience and I began our adventure as I introduced them to Mike Pasakarnis. He became more than just a name when they saw him standing life-size on the screen with a large wolf's face on his black T-Shirt. I described how Mike had approached me after my presentation and revealed that we had suffered a similar loss. A photo of a lightning bolt followed by a portrait of Susan in her Marine Corps uniform wove the initial two strands in the web linking Mike's soul to mine.

In putting together the presentation, I had decided not to reveal the details of Wolf's death at the beginning. Instead, I simply told my audience that Mike had asked me how his son could have known that he was going to die. I showed a slide with one of Barry Mack's dreamlike paintings that included the words "*The soul knows* ... " and I described the dream in which Susan came to me just before her death to assure me that she was fine.

Over the next few minutes I talked about offering Mike and Beth a reading and scheduling that session when Ty and I were traveling out west. I then described the surprise visit from Wolf when he came to me two days in advance of the appointment with his parents. I reviewed elements of that visit and showed the bar charts from Dr. Gary Schwartz that validated the accuracy of the evidence Wolf had given me.

I did the same thing with the details from the reading with Mike and Beth. I highlighted the character traits and statements from Wolf that allowed the audience to know him as a loving yet troubled young man when he walked this Earth and now as a wise and powerful soul. The last item on the list was Wolf's prophetic statement, "I'll be around."

Even though I had greatly pared down the large amount of data from both sessions, the information filled several slides. I assured the audience that Wolf's mention of things such as spirals, labyrinths, and red wagons would become very meaningful in just a few moments. I thanked them for their patience and told them there was a reason I spent so much time going over the evidence Wolf had shared from beyond the veil.

"Ladies and Gentlemen," I said, "I now want you to meet Michael Wolf Pasakarnis." I pressed the button on my remote control and revealed a photo of Wolf gazing at the viewers with his hauntingly magnetic eyes. A soft hum arose from the audience as Mike Junior now became far more than just a list of evidence on a set of slides.

"Wolf wants you to pay attention," I said and then joked, "So, if you've been nodding off until now, that's about to change."

I brought up the slide of Burial Hill and began telling the story of Wolf's final day in physical form. There was no need to embellish or add drama; the events spoke for themselves, starting from the moment Wolf abruptly rose from a conversation with his friends and said, "I have to go now."

I described the sudden appearance of a thunderstorm centered over the cemetery and its one fateful bolt out of the blue that took Wolf home. I showed the photo of the tree with the two red roses placed there by Wolf's father and step-mother when they went to the spot to pay their respects to their beloved son. I flipped to a photo of Wolf's final poem, tacked under the ceiling in the nature room where Beth had encountered it.

"Are you paying attention?" I asked again, and then zoomed in on the last line in Wolf's final poem. As those in the audience read the words, *"The time has come for the light of nature to free my soul,"* they gasped, as I knew they would. I repeated again, *"The soul knows"* and flipped to a photo of Wolf, his arms outstretched, showing off his black T-Shirt with the jagged bolt of lightning across the chest.

The stunned expressions on the faces staring at the screen told me that everyone in attendance was indeed paying attention. "But there's more," I said softly. Many in the audience now leaned forward expectantly.

The next slide showed Wolf's poem again, but this time I zoomed in on the sketch of the eye. I had drawn a circle around the yin-yang symbol at the center to temporarily hide the drawing's most notable feature.

"You will understand the importance of this yin-yang symbol in a moment," I said, "but for now, look beside the cornea." I pressed the remote and the yellow circle moved from the yin-yang symbol to the tree with two roses. Another press of the button and Mike and Beth's photo of the tree with their two roses appeared beside the sketch. Everyone in attendance now had their eyes riveted on the images. I could almost see their minds absorbing and processing the stunning details.

I then took the audience back to Virginia Beach where I showed them the labyrinth next to Wolf's matching drawing of the dolphins in the yin-yang symbol. I continued weaving the strands of the web into an intricate tapestry, sharing details about the Radio Flyer wagon, Barry Mack's *"Going Home"* painting, and the bird that flew into Wolf's bedroom window.

The congregation gasped again and then laughed with delight when I uncovered the mystery of *pajama jama mama*. I enjoyed keeping them in the dark as to why Wolf had led me to an Andean statue in a book about 2012 and the Mayan calendar. I wanted his message to be just as much a gift for them as it had been for me.

After I told them about Velvet's fulgurite necklace, not a soul laughed at my offer to leave a crystal in Lake Louise. Even those who might have approached the evening skeptically clamored in delight at the timely appearance of angel wings in the clouds after my special ceremony.

I then took them into the Starbucks coffee shop and showed them the cover of the book that Charles had presented me. I pointed out the spiral and reminded them that this was one of the first images Wolf had shared with me.

One by one I revealed the findings in Little Grandmother's book that related to things Wolf had shared in his unexpected visit. When I came to the paragraph about the Mayans and the indigenous people who are now teaching us to once again live from the heart, I displayed a collage of pictures that included the Pachamama statue and a dream catcher.

"This book and the message it revealed was the gift I had been promised," I announced as I showed a slide with a giant puzzle piece. "All of the unexplained details from Wolf's initial visit now made sense."

I noted many heads shaking in wonder when I read Little Grandmother's statement that the time of the lone wolf is over. I explained that Wolf had gone to great effort to lead me from one clue to another from the day he first made his presence known to me to the day I finally understood his message.

"We are now in a period of alignment of our solar system with the heart of the galaxy," I explained. "It is time for us to come into alignment with the center of our own little universe, right here." I tapped the center of my chest.

I showed a photo from our visit to Antelope Canyon early that summer. It featured a brilliant shaft of sunlight shining from a hole in the canyon roof to the sandy floor below. "Until Wolf came into my life," I informed my rapt audience, "I used to sit in meditation and picture a shaft of light coming down from the heavens and flowing through my body like you see in this picture.

"Wolf showed me that by focusing only on the celestial energies, I was missing half of the equation; I was therefore out of alignment. When we use our minds to visualize energy coming into our bodies from below as well as from above, we enter into a state of greater energetic balance, a theme he featured in so many of his yin-yang drawings."

I switched to a drawing of two blue whirlpools in which one of the whirlpools spiraled downward and the other upward. I focused the laser on the point in the middle where the two tips touched and said, "An interesting shape results when energy flows in a balanced manner from above as well as from below."

I brought to the screen one of the graphics that Barry Mack had created after Wolf and Sanaya showed me how to apply sacred geometry to their teachings. Barry's drawing depicted the upward and downward facing spirals overflowing like a fountain of water. The two cascades of energy merged to form a unified sphere. The resultant shape resembled a large blue donut.

"This shape is called a 'torus,'" I said. "It results when energy in an electromagnetic field flows in a balanced manner from two poles. The torus is one of the most fundamental patterns of life. It surrounds every life form from the smallest atoms to the largest galaxies.

"The flow of energy around our Earth forms the torus shape you see here." I showed a graphical depiction of the Earth with two large torus-shaped fields around it. "Lest you think this is New Age nonsense, please note where I found this drawing." I slid my laser pointer to the lower right-hand corner of the slide and drew red circles around the words, "*Courtesy of NASA.*"

The looks of surprise emanating from my audience were palpable. I had made my point.

"This is a depiction of the radiation belts that fill the space around our planet," I explained. "And what shape are they? A torus."

I pressed the remote control again as I said, "*As above, so below*. This drawing from the Heartmath Institute demonstrates the electromagnetic field produced by the human heart. Do you recognize this shape?"

Once again, my question was rhetorical. It was impossible not to see the donut-shaped field of energy centered on the heart.

"The electromagnetic field of the heart is forty to sixty times stronger than that of the brain. This field changes according to your emotions. Can you understand why you might feel unbalanced emotionally and physically if the basic energy that sustains you—your Life Force—is out of alignment?

"Wolf came to tell us that we human beings are out of alignment with our true nature. Because we place so much value today on logic, technology, and the intellect, we are neglecting the heart. As a result, we are unbalanced spiritually, prisoners of the head.

"Based on his mental state, some people might have used the term 'unbalanced' to describe Wolf. What he was lacking mentally, however, he more than made up for from the heart."

I showed one of Wolf's paintings of a bright red heart with black chains across it. "Wolf chose his nickname because the wolf symbolizes freedom. Look at the words he painted here: 'I long to be freed of the chains that hold my heart captive.'"

I once again showed a picture of a Radio Flyer wagon with the caption *"Going home,"* and I asked, "How do *you* find freedom? By balancing the head with the heart.

"The head is representative of the ego and our human nature. The ego sees only the separation between itself and other humans, but a heart-centered focus is one of unity. We are very much 'in the head' when we keep our focus on the body and the mind. At the level of the heart we see our oneness with All That Is.

"Being in the head is not necessarily bad, but focusing on our human side is only part of our wholeness. Our task is to remain aware that we walk in two worlds at once—the physical world and the world of spirit.

"Wolf Pasakarnis walked in both worlds at once. He was well aware of the constant tug of war between the heart and the head," I said as I showed another of his colorful drawings of the yin-yang symbol.

"The physical world is filled with opposites: with good and bad, pleasure and pain. As human beings we move back and forth between two poles of experience from one moment to the next, full participants in the dual nature of life in the third dimension. The problem is that we play our roles here so well that we forget that we're more than human beings and that there is more than one reality. We get stuck in our heads, sucked in by the drama, unable to see any way out.

"When you become aware that you are both a human being and a spirit being, you can then make a conscious choice to shift your awareness to the heart. From this state of higher consciousness, you become a neutral observer of what is going on at the ego level and can better decide how you will react when you return your consciousness to the role of participant.

"As difficult as it is to live in a world of opposites, there is great purpose in this physical dimension. They call our experience here 'The School of Life' for good reason. It is through our choices that we learn and grow. We find peace when we make choices that are in alignment with our true nature, which is love. The more loving our thoughts and actions are, the higher the overall state of consciousness we achieve and take back with us when we leave our physical bodies behind."

I now showed a photo of a heart-shaped stone, much like the ones Wolf used to give as gifts. "When you place your focus on the heart, you find greater understanding of why humans act the way they do toward each other. You experience greater tolerance, not just for others, but for yourself, because you realize that essentially we are all the same: beautiful souls doing our best to carry out our human roles. With that awareness comes greater patience, not just for others, but for yourself as well."

I returned to the photo of the shaft of light inside Antelope Canyon and explained that Wolf had recently shown me a way to bring our physical bodies into alignment with our spiritual selves. I invited all present to join me in a special heart meditation that would help them to experience their true nature. I waited while a staff member dimmed the lights and everyone adjusted their seats. I then turned on the CD player I had brought with me and began:

Sit quietly now with your feet flat on the floor, your arms uncrossed, your palms face up or face down in your lap. Slowly draw in a breath. Hold it for a few counts and let it out as slowly as you took it in. Take in another deep breath. Hold it, and as you release it, visualize any negativity and tension flowing out through the soles of your feet, being absorbed into the Earth. Continue relaxing more and more with the breath and feel yourself sinking deeper and deeper into your chair.

As your mind slows down and your body relaxes, visualize a shaft of white light coming from above and passing through you into the ground. Follow that shaft of light with your consciousness to the very center of the Earth. Now breathe in, and as you do so, breathe the energy of the Earth up, up, up from the center straight into your heart. Exhale normally and comfortably. Do this again, drawing in the energy from Mother Earth, from her center all the way up through the soles of your feet and into your heart. When it gets there, allow it to continue flowing throughout and beyond your body, forming a sphere of loving energy around you.

Now that you have that flow going, visualize a continuous stream from the center of the Earth to your heart. This flow replenishes and refreshes the Earth energies that make up your physical body. Feel gratitude for your life and for all of the things on this Earth with which you are blessed.

Now move your attention to the realm of Spirit. Move your consciousness high above you. As you breathe in, draw in the energy of the cosmos, that spirit energy, from as high as you can travel on the shaft of light, all the way down through your head and into your heart.

Repeat the action of inhaling from as high above as possible, drawing in with the breath the spirit energies from above directly to your heart. As that energy reaches your heart, allow it to circulate wherever it needs to go within and around your body. Visualize the flow continuing now with every breath you take.

Inhale again, and as you do so visualize the Earth energies and the celestial energies flowing in simultaneously on the breath, from below and from above, unifying at the heart. This dual stream balances the energies coming into union at the heart.

Be aware of your consciousness residing in the body, but know that this is not the only place it resides. See your body sitting within this shaft of light, but now move your consciousness above the body. Shift your awareness to a place about one foot above the head but still within the shaft of light. Visualize yourself dissolving into your natural state as a particle of light. Look down at your body. It is maintained below you on the chair, but you as spirit are everywhere at once.

Now drift down the shaft of light into your body. Flow past the head into the chest area. Feel yourself glide into that sacred heart space. How does it feel to be there? All of the energy from below and above flow and join you there. How does it feel? You can sense the head far above you and the feet far below. They are not the real you. How does the real you feel?

Dwelling with your consciousness in this sacred space, hear these words:

'Spirit of Great Healer, awaken within this heart. Peace and tranquility flow like water. May the light of All That Is free my soul and awaken me fully to the truth of who I am. I am far more than the physical body. I am without form, without limit, beyond space, beyond time. I am in everything, and everything is in me.

I am the light.

I am the light.

I am the light.'

This is alignment—this state of being in the heart, no longer prisoner to the head, but in a state of awareness of your true being ... a unified whole comprised of the Earth energies and the spirit energies. You are all of that.

Know that you can return to this place of peace, this place of tranquility, at any time. Know that here you will always be home. Return here often. This is the real you. Gratitude will bring you here instantly. Come to know it intimately as you kindle more and more the flame within you. For now, take a cleansing breath and slowly return to full waking consciousness.

I turned off the music and waited a few moments for everyone to open their eyes. Unlike the jumble of frequencies I felt within the sanctuary before the meditation, I now experienced the group's vibration as a single, peaceful hum. It felt almost disrespectful to break the silence, but I needed to move on. "How did you like that?" I asked gently. The soft murmur of approval from the audience confirmed what I was sensing from the wordless communication of their bodies.

"What you are experiencing now is a state of coherence. You have brought your mind, body, and spirit into balance and you can see how good it feels. If you don't have the time to do this heart meditation, the easiest way to achieve a state of coherence is with an expression of gratitude."

I pulled up the diagram that I had shown earlier of the torus-shaped field around the heart. "According to the Heartmath institute, feelings of gratitude, appreciation and other positive emotions synchronize brain and heart rhythms. This creates a shift to a coherent state, generating a greater balance of emotions.

"If you pay attention to your body as you mentally review all of the things for which you are thankful, you will feel a pleasant surge of energy in your chest. This balanced, coherent state allows your inner light to shine and your physical body reacts in kind."

I displayed a picture of the Earth with a sparkling energetic grid around it. "Seeing from the heart results in greater awareness of our interconnectedness. It is from this higher state of unity consciousness that we watch the drama of life unfold below us with compassion. The result is freedom from the false identification with the world of duality as our true home and a healthier balance between the ego and the spirit."

I clicked the remote and a wolf's face filled the screen. "The wolf comes when we most need guidance in our lives," I said, "and Wolf's spirit has come to us from across the veil to help us now. By pointing out our dual nature as both human beings and spirit-beings and giving us proof that both worlds exist, he has helped us to see that we learn and grow depending on whether our choices come from the head or from the heart."

I clicked my remote control and showed a black and white photo of Wolf sitting in front of the art-covered walls of his apartment and pointing at his head. I could almost hear him saying, "*It's busy in here.*"

I moved my gaze from the photo to the audience. "Wolf Pasakarnis was considered 'lesser' by our standards, but he is a more powerful soul than any other family member I have brought through from the other side in a reading. His soul knew he had fulfilled his mission here as a human being and that it was time to go to his true home. He left this dimension in a flash of light with an amazing story that demands our attention."

I clicked to a final slide showing the portrait of Wolf with his piercing eyes superimposed over a star-studded sky. With a decreasing cadence that signaled the approaching conclusion of the presentation, I said, "In his poetry, in his artwork, and in his loving actions both here and in the hereafter, Wolf left us lessons in how to access the spirit of the Great Healer."

I crossed my hands over my heart and said, "In so doing, he has shown each of us how to find peace and tranquility and to allow the light of God to free our souls."

There was a moment of silence as those gathered digested the closing words before breaking into a round of animated applause. I glanced at Ty who gave me an enthusiastic thumbs up from the back of the sanctuary. Emotion filled my heart, and I knew that I now had one more blessing for which to be grateful. Wolf had told me that his story was meant to be shared and I had done so. The dress rehearsal was over, and from the reactions I had witnessed, his message would be well received at the conference in Crete and beyond.

I raised my gaze skyward to give thanks and realized then that no one had turned the lights back up after the meditation. There was no need to. Thanks to Wolf's message, the sanctuary glowed brighter than ever.

CHAPTER SEVENTEEN

Full Circle

Life did not slow down after Ty and I returned home to Florida. A week after unpacking the coach, I flew to Greece to speak at the *"Life, Death, and Beyond"* conference with Dr. Eben Alexander and four other presenters. We were joined by forty kindred spirits, including Mike and Beth, who traveled halfway around the world to experience the mystical energy on the island of Crete.

The conference included a blend of seminars and visits to ancient sites. The trip was publicized as "a healing journey," designed to provide participants with insights, experiential techniques, and cutting-edge information to help heal and free the soul. With Wolf's emphasis on freedom, my *Heart Gifts* presentation fit perfectly with that theme.

On the morning of the second day, our group visited the archeological site of the Minoan palace of Knossos. When the tour guide informed us that we were standing on the spot of the first labyrinth in history, built for King Minos of Crete at Knossos, I exchanged a knowing glance with Mike and Beth. The rest of the group would soon understand why labyrinths were so important to the three of us. We snapped photos of the palace and the many spirals carved into large ceramic urns dating back to the Bronze Age.

After enjoying a traditional Greek lunch of moussaka, we drove high into the surrounding hills for a tour of the cave where Zeus was alleged to have been born. On the return trip to the hotel we stopped at the Greek Orthodox monastery of Kera. Our guide offered a brief tour of the monastery and then set us free to wander the grounds. At the gift shop I bought an icon of Archangel Michael and was on my way to the bus when Mike approached me. I was stunned by his sudden change in demeanor.

"Did you see what they're doing in the chapel?" he asked incredulously.

"No," I said. "What's the matter?"

"The nuns are wrapping chains around people's hearts!"

I understood immediately why he looked so shocked, and my jaw dropped. Wolf had shown me straps across my chest during my reading with his parents. Many of his drawings depicted chains around the heart. I had included one of them in the *Heart Gifts* presentation, but I had never heard of anyone actually *doing* such a thing.

"Why are they doing that?" I asked.

He shook his head in disbelief. "They're using the same chains that were used in the fourteenth century to keep the Turks from stealing an icon of the Virgin Mary. The chains are supposed to work miracles, so the nuns wrap them around people who need healing."

I did a double take as I thought about the purpose of this trip. *For healing ...*

"Can anyone do it?" I asked, my mind whirling.

"Anyone who's Greek Orthodox," Mike said with a clear edge of disappointment.

"You and Beth have to do it anyway," I insisted.

"Do you think so?" he asked tentatively.

"Yes, I do, Mike. You and I both know there are no coincidences. This is happening for a reason."

I paused then to put aside my personal feelings. Checking in with my team in spirit by shifting my consciousness and asking them if Mike and I should proceed, I sensed no discomfort. I glanced at my watch and then at the bus parked a few yards away. We were scheduled to leave in five minutes.

"Come on," I said, already in motion.

We returned to the chapel we had toured a short time earlier and entered the small, dim space. In a corner near the altar three nuns were reciting verses in Greek from an open Bible set on a wooden stand. I looked beyond them and saw Beth standing in front of the famous icon of the Virgin Mary. A pair of chains hung on two hooks to the left side of it.

Although I realized that what we were about to do might infringe upon the local tradition, I also realized that doing it would bring great healing to Mike and Beth, and healing was, after all, the purpose of the ritual. Recalling the unwritten Navy maxim to ask forgiveness instead of permission, I turned to Mike and Beth and said, "You go ahead and do it while I talk to the nuns."

They hesitated only a moment, and then Beth began wrapping the chains around Mike's chest. The oldest nun looked up and approached me with a look of concern. Although I spoke precious little Greek, I had no trouble understanding her use of the word, "*Orthodox?*"

Standing my ground between her and Mike and Beth, I mustered as much love as I could. I held the nun's eyes as I held out my arms to her. "They lost their son," I said from the heart.

The nun frowned and took a step forward. I glanced behind me and saw that Mike had removed the chains and was now wrapping them around Beth. I knew the nun couldn't understand what I was saying, but I hoped that the sincerity in my voice would convey the importance of what Mike and Beth were doing. I mimicked the motions of cradling a baby in my arms and then pointed at Mike and Beth. "Their lost their son," I repeated, then pointed upward and said, "He's in Heaven now. This is for their healing."

We may not have spoken the same language, but Spirit speaks without words. Somehow my meaning got through to her. She nodded her head, made the sign of the cross, and turned away to rejoin her sisters.

I walked to where Mike and Beth now stood in front of the icon. Both had tears in their eyes.

"You should do it, too," Mike said.

I glanced at my watch and then at the nun, and suddenly nothing mattered but the present moment.

"What do I do?" I asked.

Mike and Beth each took one of the sacred chains and helped me to crisscross them over my back. They handed the ends to me and I brought them together at my heart.

"Now you're supposed to kiss the painting," Mike said.

Wolf's words echoed in my mind: *"I long to be free of the chains that hold my heart captive."* Tears flowed freely as I leaned in and touched my lips to the cool glass protecting the Blessed Mary.

I straightened, wiped my eyes, and lifted the heavy links from my back. With Mike and Beth's help, we hung them carefully on the set of hooks next to the sacred icon. With our hands held as if in prayer, we bowed and thanked the nuns before stepping out of the dimly lit chapel into dazzling sunshine.

Most of our group was already on the bus when we returned to the parking lot, although a few stragglers remained in the gift shop. We stood beside the door, breathless, not from the brisk walk to the bus, but from the wonder of such a surreal experience. When the driver announced that it was time to depart, we wiped our eyes once again and climbed aboard.

I slipped into my seat and stared out the window, lost in thought. One of my fellow travelers peeked around from the seat behind mine and asked, "Are you okay?"

"More than you know," I replied.

"It looked like you three had some kind of special moment back there."

"We sure did," I said, "And I'll tell you all about it tomorrow. After you hear the *Heart Gifts* presentation, it will make much more sense."

The next day I delivered my presentation as scheduled. By this time, everyone in the group knew each other fairly well. During the past few days we had meditated together, broken bread together, and enjoyed interesting sights and presentations. The atmosphere was relaxed and comfortable. When I began my slideshow with a picture of Dr. Alexander standing with me at the conference in Virginia Beach, the audience smiled at the sight of him seated with them today in Greece.

As I switched to a picture of Mike in his Wolf's T-Shirt at that same conference, I could see looks of curiosity on their faces. By this time, most everyone knew that Mike and Beth had lost a son named Wolf, but they had no idea that Mike, Beth, and Wolf would play starring roles in my presentation. I could sense the interest growing as I launched into the story.

A presentation that had been exceedingly well received in St. Louis took on a different feel in Crete. The energy I received from this group was one of reverence as I shared the details of Wolf's death and his subsequent efforts to assure us that those on the other side remain close to us.

When I reached the point in the presentation where I discuss sacred geometry, I displayed a slide that I had added that morning. It showed a photograph of one of the urns we had seen on our tour of Knossos the day before. "We saw many examples of spirals yesterday," I said. "Since ancient times, spirals have represented spiritual growth and the ever-expanding journey of the soul."

Gesturing toward Dr. Alexander in the audience, I said, "Many people who have had near-death experiences recall traveling down a tunnel toward a bright light. Dr. Alexander described the tunnel more like a spiral leading to what he called 'the core.'"

I looked around the conference room at my group of new friends and asked pointedly, "What is the core of you?"

Several people answered, "The heart."

I nodded. "Yes," I said. "It is the heart."

When I came to Wolf's drawing of the heart with chains around it, I deviated from the prepared presentation and shared what had occurred the day before in the chapel at Kera. Now the group understood why Mike, Beth, and I had been so emotional when we returned to the bus. I noticed several people swiping at tears. Having come to know Mike and Beth so well in recent days made Wolf's story that much more meaningful to them.

A number of those in attendance had suffered the loss of a child. They came to the conference in search of answers and the healing that the brochures had promised. By the end of the presentation, the tears emanating from almost everyone in the audience clearly demonstrated the presence and blessing of true healing.

I looked at Beth and Mike. Beth's face was contorted as she struggled to control her emotions. I crossed the room to her and we hugged as she wept openly and people gathered around. Standing back to let others embrace her and Mike, I marveled once again at how Wolf had brought the three of us together.

We had met at a conference where a spiral-shaped labyrinth mirrored one of their son's drawings. Now, after an unexpected but magical journey with Wolf, we were together at another conference in another country where the shape of the spiral featured prominently in its culture. In between the two conferences, Wolf had helped me to piece together an intricate puzzle of interconnecting parts that, once made whole, revealed an extraordinary image of love, hope and eternity, and what that image means for us as both physical and spiritual beings.

All around me the audience chattered reverentially about the evidence Wolf had brought through from the other side, each member convinced now more than ever that there truly is life after death and that our departed loved ones never leave us. Many expressed a newfound resolve to more closely monitor the signs that those in the spirit world often put before us. They marveled at how I was able to piece together the puzzle with the seemingly discordant clues Wolf had provided.

I felt immense satisfaction as I packed up my slides, but now I was ready to relax. I left the conference room and walked down the stone path toward my hotel room, reflecting that Mike, Beth, and I had come full circle from Virginia Beach to Crete. I had forgotten, however, that our life on this earth unfolds like a spiral. The journey of the soul is ever onward, ever upward. I may have pieced together all of the pieces of Wolf's puzzle, but what I didn't realize at that moment was that I hadn't yet seen the whole picture.

"I'll be around," Wolf had said, and he was right.

The journey wasn't quite over.

CHAPTER EIGHTEEN

Tying It All Together

With the Florida sun nudging temperatures to the upper seventies, I gratefully removed my winter gloves and other wintry clothing items from my suitcase and stored them on the top shelf of my closet. A quick trip to the nation's capital had reminded me, yet again, why Ty and I choose to spend winters in Florida. In spite of the frigid weather in the Upper South, it was well worth the effort to fly there. The large crowd at Unity of Fairfax in Oakton, Virginia responded with the same enthusiasm to my *Heart Gifts* presentation as did all those with whom I had shared Wolf's story.

In the four months since returning from Crete I had presented *Heart Gifts* at the worldwide headquarters for Unity in Kansas City, Missouri, and at a variety of locations in Florida, including the large First Unity at Unity Campus in St. Petersburg. After my presentation there, spiritual leader Reverend Temple Hayes invited me to return at a later date and participate on a panel of "women visionaries." I agreed, having no idea that it would involve a stunning connection with Wolf.

It was through that panel that I met author and spiritual teacher Janet Conner. Intrigued by our similar belief systems, I bought her latest book, *The Lotus and the Lily.* Her central message that we create our ideal life not by asking God to provide us what we want, but by creating the right conditions within ourselves to be an instrument of Spirit is one I hold close to my heart.

Fascinated to find a discussion of sacred geometry in the introduction, I underlined a quote by the Sufi poet Hafiz: "*I have gotten the hint: There is something about circles.*" The words triggered a memory of the moment during Mike and Beth's reading when I found myself moving my pen in circles, as though my motions were guided by an outside force.

The introduction to *The Lotus and the Lily* featured a discussion of mandalas. Up to now, I had thought that the word "mandala" referred only to the circular designs used by Buddhists and Hindus to enhance meditation. I was surprised to read in Janet's book, however, that mandala means "circle" in the Sanskrit language and can refer to any kind of circles used for any purpose.

My interest in mandalas increased even more when I turned a page and encountered a drawing of a spiral-shaped seashell. I felt a growing excitement at finding spiritual concepts in Janet's book that supported the bases of my *Heart Gifts* presentation. Upon reading a few more lines, my excitement shifted to astonishment when Janet discussed the use of circles to express the union of the human and the divine. "The Native American medicine wheel ... the labyrinth ... the yin-yang symbol—," she wrote, "—all are mandalas."

I went back and reread the list: Native Americans, wheels, labyrinths, and yin-yang symbols. Each of these items had captured my attention and my imagination from the moment Wolf entered my life. To find them all in the same sentence of this book had to be more than mere chance.

I went online and ordered two books Janet had recommended: *Mandala*, by Jose and Miriam Arguelles, and *Mandala: Journey to the Center*, by Bailey Cunningham. The former was an older book published by Shambala Press, the latter a more contemporary full-color volume published by Dorling Kindersley. The moment I placed the order, I experienced a peaceful feeling that told me I need do no further research at that point. Trusting Spirit, I resolved to put aside all thoughts of mandalas until the two books arrived.

I was pleased to find them waiting for me on the kitchen table when I returned from my trip to Washington. With my bags unpacked and the dinner table cleared, I settled on the couch with the books. I briefly studied each one trying to determine which I should read first. Like most Dorling Kindersley publications, Cunningham's book was filled with visually appealing full-color photos and diagrams.

I began with the foreword to that book and soon found connections with Wolf's message when the author linked mandalas with wholeness and finding peace. Moving on to the introduction, I underlined a sentence that mirrored what Janet Conner had written in her book about the various types of symbols used for mandalas: "The thread that weaves together what may seem at first to be unrelated images and concepts," Cunningham wrote, "is the circle, the mandala."

I suddenly felt lightheaded as a voice in my head shouted, *"Missing piece! Missing piece!"*

I recognized Wolf's presence and mentally replied, *"I thought I had found all the missing pieces."*

In response, the urge to continue reading increased in intensity. Farther down the page I discovered a quote attributed to the Dalai Lama. I knew by the words of that quote that Wolf had intended for me to find the information in the book. The Dalai Lama referred to a mandala as "an optical mechanism which can be used by anyone to discover *freedom.*"

I was prepared to turn the page and begin reading Part One, when Wolf guided me to switch books. I opened the Arguelles book and was struck by the similarity between the black and white drawings there and Wolf's many sketches. Fascinated, I turned a few more pages and stopped short. With a distinct feeling of deja-vu , I beheld a full-page mandala with an eye at the center. Just like the eye that accompanied Wolf's final poem, this one had a yin-yang symbol where the pupil would normally be. The description stated that the pupil of the eye is a simple mandala representing the bridge between the outer light of the physical world and the light that burns within us.

"Now do you see why I included the eye?" Wolf asked.

I was beginning to see, but a sense of urgency that left me feeling hyper-alert told me there was still more to learn. I wondered if I would be able to sleep before finishing both books.

"Talk about the target," Wolf now whispered, repeating a phrase he had said to me during the reading with his parents.

I shook my head in confusion.

"Go back and look at the transcript," he said.

His instructions were so clear that I set the books aside and went to my study to retrieve the transcript of Mike and Beth's reading. I returned with it to the couch and began flipping through the pages until I came to the word "target." Wolf had spoken of it when he showed me several archery symbols. Earlier, Mike had confirmed that his brother had given Wolf a bow and arrow and had taught him how to shoot. At the time, I had assumed that Wolf was simply sharing a memory of one of his hobbies. Activities that those in spirit form enjoyed while in human form often come through as evidence in a reading.

"*He just showed me a target, like 'bingo,'*" I had said to Mike and Beth at the time. Re-reading the transcript now, I recalled wondering why I had used the word "bingo." It is not a word I normally use. My friend Lynn Spence had also uncharacteristically used the same word after she solved the mystery of the Radio Flyer wagon.

"I'm supposed to talk about the target," I had said during the reading, but once Mike confirmed that Wolf enjoyed archery, I spoke no more about it.

"*The key is in there,*" Wolf said now, and in my mind's eye I saw a finger pointing. "*At the center of the target. Now go back and look at the mandalas.*"

I set the transcript aside and returned to the Arguelles book. I turned a page and my gaze was drawn like a magnet to a mandala consisting of a series of concentric circles with a bull's eye center that looked exactly like an archery target.

"*Bingo!*" said Wolf. "*Everything goes back to the center. Read the transcript again.*"

I did as instructed and suddenly saw with great clarity how hard Wolf had worked to bring circles to my attention. He had inundated me with examples of objects with wheels, showing me images of bicycles, skateboards, and red wagons. "*It's really about the wheels,*" I had said, "*and now I see a pair of roller skates. Wheels, wheels, wheels. It's about the wheels.*"

I realized then that the word "mandala" was not in my conscious mind when Wolf initially visited me. He may have tried to whisper "*mandala*" in my ear, but if he had, I didn't hear it. He had no choice but to speak of circles, spirals, planets, and wheels, in hopes that I would eventually grasp the point he was trying to make.

"*I think he's trying to show you the big picture here,*" I said during the reading when I found myself drawing circles. "*It's all about the oneness.*"

I laid the transcript on my lap and stared into space. My words showed that I had seen the big picture during the reading, but afterward I became sidetracked by focusing on the unsolved evidence from his initial visit. Uncovering the missing pieces of the puzzle had revealed an important message about bringing mind and heart into alignment, but without this final key, I now realized, my *Heart Gifts* presentation was itself out of balance.

I glanced down at the cover of the DK book and did a double-take when I read the subtitle, *Journey to the Center.* I had not realized that these were the same words I had used in the introduction to my presentation. I had promised my audiences that I was going to take them on a "journey to the center" of their individual universe—the heart. Now I understood that Wolf wanted me to complete the journey by shifting the focus back to our oneness with each other.

"When you focus on your roles as human beings, you see yourselves as individual entities, like separate pieces of a puzzle. When you see with the eyes of the soul, you see the whole picture. There is only one Spirit, but it takes many forms. The center of each of you is the heart, but together you form the one heart of God. As above, so below.

"This understanding is what is most needed at this time so that all of you may find freedom," Wolf whispered to me now. "You find your way home through the heart."

I sat back against the couch, stunned by these powerful lessons. They were not new to me, but the way Wolf had led me to find them shook me to the core. It was clear that he had no intention of letting me be until I recognized the significance of mandalas. I took a deep breath and as I slowly exhaled, I realized that I no longer felt agitated. The urge to read further was gone.

I set the books aside and glanced at the clock. It was late, but I decided to check emails before going to bed. As I quickly scanned the list of new messages, I concluded that most of them could wait until morning. But one name stood out. I had enjoyed Cindy Evart's company just the day before when she had driven from her home in West Virginia to attend my *Heart Gifts* presentation at Unity of Fairfax. Cindy and I had met through our mutual friend, Lynn Spence. I helped Cindy to connect with her beloved son, Tristan, who had passed to the other side at age sixteen as the result of a fatal car accident.

The subject of Cindy's email read, *"Thank you for a great day."* Intrigued, I opened her email and started reading.

"I wanted to make sure you know how much your message has been a part of my healing and transformative journey over the past few years," Cindy wrote. She then commented on my *Heart Gifts* presentation. "Thank you for helping me to draw my attention to the absolute miracles found in day-to-day signs. I receive so many of those little signs that I was beginning to take them for granted. You helped me to re-gain a little of that wonder."

She went on to share some of the gifts that Tristan sends her from the other side. One gift was to lead her to find a perfect heart-shaped rock just like the ones Wolf used to give to friends.

"Oh, and one more thing," Cindy wrote. "As my daughter and I were driving home yesterday, we saw a billboard that made us smile. We took a picture, which I have attached. I hope it also gives you a smile."

I clicked on the attachment and when it opened on my computer screen the first thing I noticed was the gray sky so typical of a winter's day in Virginia. When I focused on the billboard standing in a snowy field, I gasped. The message from a local church was a clever imitation of the "*Got milk?*" commercials often seen on television in recent years. Instead of a face with a milky mustache, however, the sign featured a large red wagon with the "Radio Flyer" brand name on the side. Next to the wagon were two simple words inscribed in large letters: "*Got freedom?*"

Now I not only smiled, I laughed with joy at how the Universe works. The message of freedom alongside a Radio Flyer wagon and the timing of its arrival in light of Wolf's mandala revelations were nothing short of miraculous. What Cindy didn't know was that the Radio Flyer mystery had been solved by our mutual friend Lynn Spence. If Lynn or I had harbored any doubts that Wolf had summoned the wagon as a vehicle to symbolize his keen desire to "go home," Cindy's unexpected gift confirmed it.

My ever patient husband had remained quiet throughout the evening while I hastily highlighted passages in my two new books and gasped at Cindy's email. I shared my findings with him while we got ready for bed, and he listened with amazement.

"Are you going to be able to sleep?" he asked as we crawled under the covers.

"I think so," I replied.

We kissed goodnight and I turned out the light. As I laid back and stared up at the ceiling, I thought about the first time that Wolf had made his presence known to me. He had come in the early morning hours when my mind is most receptive to those in spirit. I closed my eyes and sent him a special request. "*If there is anything else I need to know or a way you can bring this all together, please visit me in the night.*"

I rolled onto my left side and Ty snuggled up behind me. Trying not to move too much, I reached out to make sure my notepad and pen were on the nightstand. Feeling the smoothness of the paper under my fingers, I pulled my hand back and wrapped it around Ty's hand before drifting off to sleep.

At 3:30 Wolf awakened me. His presence was unmistakable and far clearer than when I sensed him in full waking consciousness. I pulled my notebook to my side and lay with pen poised to write.

He began by reminding me of his first two visits. Both times, the first things he had shown me were shapes, drawings, and hieroglyphics. *"That was for a reason,"* he said now. *"There was meaning in the fact that I got straight to the point with symbols."*

He flashed before my eyes the paper with his final poem and the drawing of the eye. *"Everything was symbolic,"* he said, and I underlined the word *"everything."*

"The whole thing, including the eye and all of its symbolism, is about knowing yourself as spirit and understanding your oneness with your Source."

As if to make sure I didn't miss a single piece of meaning, he went through the poem line by line, beginning with, *"Spirit of Great Healer, awaken from within this heart."*

"The heart is the center point, your true home, the place to find freedom," he said, before showing me the monastery in Crete where the nuns used the chains for healing. *"The first line is about healing the heart of mankind."*

I wrote down the second line of the poem as he recited it: *"Peace and tranquility flow like water,"* Wolf said, and then: *"This will be the outcome, once all of you begin to heal."*

He reminded me of the final line of his poem, *"The time has come to allow the light of nature to free my soul,"* and he stated, *"For me, it was a lightning bolt that freed my soul. It is the light of the Great Healer at the center of each of you that will lead you home."*

Now he drew my attention to his drawing of the eye. *"Look at each of the pieces, and you will see how they all fit together."*

He began with the dream catcher to the left of the pupil. He focused on the circular web in the center, pointing out that it was yet another example of a mandala. *"I drew this to show the interconnectedness of all of you with each other and with All That Is.*

"Now look at the center of the eye with the yin-yang mandala," he said. *"This symbol of balance and harmony also represents wholeness. It represents the integrated self."*

And finally he showed me the tree with the two roses on the right side of his sketch. *"This gives you proof that my soul existed in two worlds at once. I placed this drawing in an eye so that you will see yourselves as both spirit beings and human beings at once."*

Wolf then tied all of the pieces together by reminding me that the eye, by itself, was symbolic of the bridge between the outer light of the physical world and the inner light of our spirit-nature.

I wrote down his words as fast as I could, amazed at the revelation that what I had thought were three distinct sketches within the eye were each deliberately placed there to convey one cohesive message.

"Now do you see why the eye is so critical?" he asked, and I did. Not one facet of his depiction was drawn randomly.

He laughed and recited lines from the poem he had dictated to me when I was in Alberta, Canada. *"The answers were there, hidden in plain sight. They came to you at night when you wrote without a light."*

"Yes," I nodded, astounded by the realization. They were hidden in his drawing of an eye ... *in plain sight.*

"For it's all a great big web, which is what has oft been said," he reminded me, and showed me Cindy Evart's photo of the billboard with the Radio Flyer wagon and its message of freedom.

"Now you see what it means to be free," Wolf said, once again reciting his poem. *"Just relax now, settle back, as your desires you attack, and the ego you release, this is the road to peace."* The words flowed as freely in the dark as they had that morning when I heard them during my meditation.

"You had all of the pieces," he said, *"but not the whole picture. You came full circle from the time you met Mike and Beth. Now go to the center. That is the target. That is where you find wholeness. Teach the message of balance as you have been doing, but tie it all together now with the lesson of oneness."*

He showed me the inside of his apartment, where the walls, ceilings, and even his furniture were covered with the creative expressions of a busy and divinely creative mind. The world was Wolf's canvas.

"I wrote poetry and drew pictures with symbols. Poetry and art, just like hieroglyphics and mandalas, are a universal method of communicating. They speak to all people everywhere because they speak to the heart, where the one Truth resounds: All ... is ... One."

I felt his powerful presence begin to withdraw. I didn't want him to go. I didn't want to break the link. I wanted to hear more, to enjoy his loving energy longer, but I sensed that he had shared all that he had come to share.

"*I see now,*" I said as my heart overflowed. "*I see.*"

"*Bingo,*" Wolf said as he pointed at the center of my chest and faded away.

THE END

Afterword

What you have just read is a true story. The dialogues with Wolf were taken verbatim either from the recorded transcripts of his visits or from my written notes. All the events happened as described and every piece of evidence is real. Why do I place such emphasis on evidence? Because as physical beings we hunger for hope. We want to know that this life is not all there is. We want to know that our deceased loved ones remain with us. We want proof that we are part of something greater than ourselves and that we are fully supported by a loving Universe.

Wolf has given us that. It is his gift to us all.

Were it not for the evidence, those who hear Wolf's story might question information emanating from the spirit world. Some skeptics might ask, "Is it all in your mind?" To them I reply, yes, of course it is, but not just in *my* mind. It is in *all* our minds. How else would those in the spirit realm be able to communicate with us? They often put thoughts into our head to guide us, and when the opportunity arises, they combine their communications with empirical evidence.

Wolf has taken multiple opportunities to demonstrate how intricately interconnected the physical world is to the spiritual world. I have saved one of the most stunning stories until the end of this book. Just like the roses he drew beside the beech tree where he knew he would be killed, the events I share with you now prove that we are multi-dimensional beings connected by consciousness and inspired by love.

It happened on the way home from giving my *Heart Gifts* presentation in Sarasota, Florida. I was driving the coach and my mind was wandering. I got to thinking about a book I had been working on for several months about attuning to higher consciousness. I had written 45,000 words, and I was debating if I should include a chapter about Wolf at the end.

Seemingly from out of nowhere, the thought occurred to me to put the *Heart Gifts* presentation into its own book. I found the idea intriguing, but I was unsure if there was enough material for a full-length manuscript. I tried to imagine the size of a book that would result from telling Wolf's story.

"*It would have to be a small book,*" I thought. "*Maybe a small hardcover book like 'Tuesdays with Morrie.'*" I visualized the best-selling book by author Mitch Albom that measured only five by seven inches. I had read it ten years earlier and although I enjoyed it immensely, I had not thought of it since.

Even though I did not sense Wolf's presence, I wondered if he might have been responsible for this unexpected idea popping into my mind. Knowing that those on the other side are always as close as our thoughts, I silently said, "*Okay, Wolf, if I'm supposed to set aside my current writing project and write your story instead, I'm going to need a sign.*"

For something as important as writing a full-length book, I wanted to have no doubt about the direction I should take. Understanding that our unseen helpers don't mind when we put them to the test, I added, "*It has to be a big sign, and I need it within twenty-four hours if it's going to count.*"

With that, I put aside all thoughts of my request.

Two hours later, after we dropped the coach off in the storage lot, we drove our Honda to our neighborhood postal station to pick up the mail. Ty waited in the car while I went to the mail box. My eyes lighted up when I drew out a large priority envelope addressed to me from Mike and Beth. During the past few months they had sent me several unexpected gifts, and from the bulky feel of the package, I assumed that here was yet another surprise.

I returned to the car and tore open the envelope as Ty backed out of the parking space. My gasps don't normally affect him these days, but the one I let out when I opened Mike and Beth's gift caused him to slam on the brakes. The five-by-seven-inch book in my hands might have held no meaning for him, but it held a heart-full of meaning for me. It confirmed not only that Wolf had received my message, but that the publication of *Wolf's Message* had the full backing of the spirit world.

Mike and Beth had sent me a copy of *The First Phone Call from Heaven*, the new release by Mitch Albom, author of *Tuesdays with Morrie.*

Synchronicities like this happen because all minds are connected. What we think are our own thoughts are often put there by our unseen helpers. I know now that Wolf gave me the idea to write his story. He then prompted me to ask for a very specific sign, knowing that the sign was waiting for me in my mailbox. I can see him rubbing his hands together and thinking, *"This ought to be good,"* as I opened the package.

This begs the question: are any of our thoughts our own? My answer is the key message I hope you take from this book: Spirit is indivisible. In truth, there is only One Mind. The words to this book flowed like water because I did not write them alone. They were divinely inspired and guided.

Some people might think I'm a bit out of my mind for talking to spirits, but the evidence speaks for itself. It has often been a dizzying experience, but it has *always* been an immense honor to travel with Wolf on this magical journey. I don't believe he was crazy. He simply walked in two worlds at once.

Wolf showed only compassion for others. He came back from the other side to show all of us that beyond our human imperfections we are pure spirit beings and our true essence is love. The reason we are here is very simple: We are here to love each other.

Acknowledgments

I give my heartfelt love and gratitude to:

- The Source of all that is ... to God, the Great Spirit, for Life itself.
- Mike and Beth Pasakarnis for your friendship, your love, and for allowing me to share your son with the world
- My husband Ty for your never-ending love and your support of me and this important work
- My dear friend and former agent, Bill Hammond, for your gift of polishing these words so that Wolf's message shines even brighter
- Dr. Gary Schwartz, for your gift to this work and to all humanity
- My agent Bill Gladstone for your support and faith in this book
- My step-daughter Elisabeth Giesemann for your outstanding cover design
- All of you who allowed me to write about your role in sharing Wolf's message: Maureen Hancock, Lynn Walker, Gail Grossman, Barry Mack, Charles Cunis, Lynn and Bailey Spence, Velvet Phillips-Sullivan, Terri Horsmann, Marigene De Rusha, Anne Gehman, Temple Hayes, and Cindy Evarts

And most certainly, this book would not exist were it not for Michael Wolf Pasakarnis – one very persistent and powerful soul. You are deeply loved.

APPENDIX A

Statistical Analysis of Wolf Pre-Reading with Suzanne Giesemann

Gary E. Schwartz, Phd

Introduction

To have people formally score readings they have had with a medium and then have the results statistically analyzed serves the cause of both humanity and science. This statement becomes especially relevant if the reading performed by the medium happens to be a "pre-reading," by which I mean the following:

(1) The reading is *spontaneous* and *unexpected*,

(2) The reading occurs *prior* to the actual reading with the "sitter" (the family member(s) wishing to hear from his or her deceased loved one(s);

(3) The medium receives *no feedback* while receiving the information (since the sitter is not present at the reading to confirm or deny that information).

What is unique about this pre-reading is that the medium (Suzanne) received apparent communication from the "deceased" (Wolf) requesting that she should have this unanticipated pre-reading carefully scored by his parents (Mike and Beth) using the standardized procedure developed in my laboratory at the University of Arizona.

Moreover, Suzanne introduced the "future" sitters (Mike and Beth) to the scoring procedures by emailing them a draft of an appendix I prepared for a book written by Janis Heaphy titled *The Hand on the Mirror*. This appendix reported the procedures and results of a highly accurate reading performed by Suzanne that focused on Janis's deceased husband Max.

What this means for Suzanne's pre-reading with Wolf is that although Mike and Beth were "novice" scorers, they were not "naïve." They understood the importance of being careful and accurate, and they had an excellent example of responsible scoring to use as their guide.

In order to estimate what I refer to as "control values" for a deceased person, it is essential to have the sitters score the same items as applied to another person other than the deceased. After Mike and Beth completed the formal scoring for Wolf, at my request Suzanne asked Mike and Beth if they would be willing to re-score the information for a "control" person whom they knew well and who was of the same sex and approximate age as Wolf when he died. Mike and Beth selected a cousin who was two years younger than Wolf. Since the control scoring was performed two years after Wolf died, the cousin was the same age as Wolf (29) when Wolf died.

Procedures

Here is how I explained the 0 – 6 rating system to Janis in my email to her. This same system was used by Mike and Beth.

0 = **the item cannot be scored** (i.e. the rater does not have the necessary information to make an honest and fair rating)

1 = **a clear miss** (i.e. the information provided by the medium is inaccurate as applied to the deceased person)

2 = **a stretch** (i.e. the information vaguely fits the deceased)

3 = **possible fit** (i.e. the information could fit the deceased)

4 = **probable fit** (i.e. the information could be interpreted as being a genuine fit / hit, but it is not completely clear)

5 = **a clear hit** (i.e. the information can easily be scored as being accurate – i.e. the fit is obvious)

6 = **a super hit** (i.e. the information is especially meaningful and significant, in addition to be clearly accurate)

In addition to rating each item presented between 0 – 6, Mike and Beth were asked to provide a one sentence explanation or justification for each rating. I could thus confirm that they were reliably and responsibly following the instructions and carefully considering each rating. In sum, the explanations provided by Mike and Beth confirmed that they had diligently followed the instructions

As you can imagine, this procedure not only took a substantial number of hours, it also took an emotional toll of them. As mentioned above, the scoring was completed first for Wolf, and then for a cousin serving as the control.

Results

There were a total of 58 items from the pre-reading which potentially could be scored for Wolf and his cousin / control.

The table below presents the summary of the scoring of Wolf versus his cousin.

Rating	Wolf	Cousin
0	12	22
1	6	29
2	2	2
3	4	3
4	10	2
5	15	0
6	9	0

As you can see, for the "O" ratings, 12 out of 58 items (20.7 percent) could not be scored by Mike and Beth for Wolf, and 22 of those same items (37.9 percent) could not be scored for the cousin.

One would predict that Mike and Beth know their son, Wolf, better than they know his cousin. The percent scores (20.7 percent versus 37.9 percent) for "0" ratings are consistent with this prediction. Also, it is apparent that Mike and Beth were careful to give scores of 1 through 6 only for those items for which they had the requisite knowledge to make a rating.

Hence, 46 items could be rated for Wolf, and 36 items could be rated for the cousin.

For ratings of "1," only thirteen percent of items were rated as "certain misses" for Wolf, whereas 80.5 percent were rated as certain misses for the cousin. These summary scores clearly indicate that relatively few items were clearly wrong for Wolf, whereas a significant majority of the items were clearly wrong for the cousin.

This is quite remarkable given the fact that this was a "pre-reading" – spontaneous, unexpected, and without any feedback from Mike and Beth at the time the information was received.

By contrast, for the ratings of 5 and 6 ("clear hits"), Wolf received an impressive score of 52.2 percent, whereas his cousin received a score of zero. These conservative summary scores clearly indicate that more than half of the items were definite hits for Wolf, whereas none of the items was rated as a definite hit for the cousin.

The reason I define these as "conservative" summary scores is because no credit was given for items rated as "4" (probable hits). For Wolf, 10 of 46 items (21.7 percent) were rated as probable hits, whereas for the cousin, only 2 of 36 items were rated as probable hits.

When we add the "probable" hits to the "clear" hits, the total percentage jumps to 73.5 percent for Wolf compared to 5.6 percent for the cousin. This comparison provides a more precise summary of the accuracy of the pre-reading for Wolf versus his cousin.

Following is a bar graph of this summary.

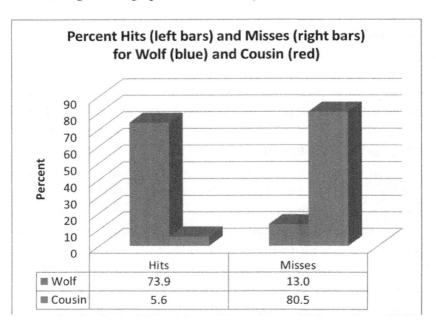

Percent Hits (left bars) and Misses (right bars) for Wolf (blue) and Cousin (red)

	Hits	Misses
Wolf	73.9	13.0
Cousin	5.6	80.5

When the ratings of 1-6 summarized in the table are submitted to statistical analysis using what is called a "t test," the following results are obtained.

	Mean	Std.Dv.	N	Diff.	Std.Dv.	t	df	p
Wolf "1-6"	3.970588	1.678479						
Cousin "1-6"	1.411765	0.891633	34	2.558824	2.062525	7.234033	33	0.000000

Since most readers are not scientists, what is important to understand from this table is that the probability of the difference between the scoring for Wolf versus the cousin as being explainable as "chance" is less than one in a million (p<.0000001). By contrast, the required criteria for statistical significance used in psychological research is less than one in twenty (p<.05).

Hence, the t test for the Wolf versus cousin data is statistically significant at the highest level.

Also critical to note is that among the "clear" hits (those with a rating of 5 or 6) 9 of 24 total items were rated as "6." This indicates that more than a third of the clear hits were "super" hits of deep meaning and significance to Mike and Beth. This would be a very high percentage of "super" hits in a normal reading; it is extraordinary for a "pre-reading."

In sum, Mike and Beth's analysis of Suzanne's reading presented in chapters 5 and 6 is supported by both sophisticated scientific scoring and statistical analysis. We therefore can be confident that Mike and Beth documented a highly accurate and meaningful pre-reading between Suzanne and their son, Wolf.

A Note to Skeptical Readers

If you become skeptical when reading this kind of book, you should understand that these analyses cannot (and should not) be dismissed as being based on ratings performed by naïve judges. In addition, these findings cannot (and should not) be dismissed as being based upon vague or general information (e.g. comparing the scoring for Wolf versus the cousin / control). Finally, this pre-reading cannot (and should not) be dismissed as the result of fraud. Such arguments are completely without merit in this instance. The scientific evidence is simply too overwhelming.

Although these findings do not by themselves "prove" that Suzanne was communicating with Wolf, they are entirely consistent with the scientific data. When other evidence presented in this book is taken into account, a compelling argument can be made that Wolf's efforts to communicate with us through Suzanne deserve to be taken seriously and Received with gratitude, awe, and celebration.

Gary E. Schwartz, PhD is professor of Psychology, Medicine, Neurology, Psychiatry, and Surgery at the University of Arizona. He is also the Chairman of Eternea (www.eternea.org). His books include *The Afterlife Experiments, The G.O.D. Experiments, The Energy Healing Experiments,* and *The Sacred Promise.*

About the Author

Suzanne Giesemann is an author, a spiritual teacher, and an evidential medium. A retired U.S. Navy Commander, she served as a commanding officer, as special assistant to the Chief of Naval Operations, and as Aide to the chairman of the Joint Chiefs of Staff. Suzanne's gift of communication with those on the other side provides stunning evidence of life after death. In her work, Suzanne addresses questions about the purpose of life, the nature of reality, and attuning to higher consciousness. The story of her transition to her current work is told in her book, *Messages of Hope: The Metaphysical Memoir of a Most Unexpected Medium*. For more information about Suzanne visit www.LoveAtTheCenter.com

A portion of the proceeds from *Wolf's Message* are donated to the Renewing Hope for Humanity Project of Eternea, a global educational and outreach organization dedicated to inspiring transformation in human nature and civilization. Chaired by Dr. Gary E. Schwartz, Ph.D., Eternea sponsors and advances scientific research and public education about spiritually transformative experiences and the nature of consciousness. Eternea's programs aim to further awareness and acceptance of the premise that the eternal continuation of consciousness is a fundamental reality. Suzanne Giesemann is the Chairman of Eternea's Spirituality Leadership Council. For information about Eternea and to find out how you can help to further the organization's mission visit www.Eternea.org

Made in the USA
Las Vegas, NV
19 May 2024

90100989R00108